The Lesbian and Gay

ALMANAC

and EVENTS of

1990

An *ENVOY* Book
Chicago

Acknowledgements

A special thank you to Barry McDell and the Metropolitan Vancouver Athletic and Arts Association for their invaluable assistance in helping gather research material for the special Gay Games section.

We also extend a special thank you to Roy M. Coe, for graciously allowing us to reproduce photographs from his book, *A Sense of Pride: The Story of Gay Games II.*

ISBN: 0-945043-02-3

CONTENTS

Lesbian and Gay Almanac of Current Events

Events of 1990

STAFF

Editor and Publisher, Danni Munson
Copy Editor, Waldemar Bojczuk
Director, Manufacturing and Production, Tom Myles

Contributing Writers:

Richard Dopson, Director of International Outreach for Gay Games III, Metropolitan Vancouver Athletic and Arts Association
Jane Troxell, Editor of Lambda Rising Book Report
Christine Riddiough, Executive Director, Gay and Lesbian Democrats of America
Rev. Sandi Robinson, Director of Ecumenical Ministry, Universal Fellowship of Metropolitan Community Churches

Correspondents:

Antique Auto Clubs: Doug Buhrer
Black and White Men Together and other Minority Events: Ollie Lee Taylor
Bowling: Lee Bowman and Ron Keel
Gay and Lesbian Pride Organizations: Richard Pfeiffer
Rodeos: Joseph Olney

ALMANAC

of Current Gay/Lesbian History

Special Gay Games Section

Event of the Year (1989)

Gay/Lesbian Year In Review

(October 1988 through September 1989)

Photo: Scott McLennan

HISTORY OF THE GAY GAMES

by Richard Dopson,
Director of International Outreach,
Metropolitan Vancouver Athletic and Arts Association

It is the memory of the Opening Ceremonies of the first Gay Games that I will always cherish. We milled around for hours outside San Francisco's Kezar Stadium, laughing, chatting and snapping photos of athletes from all over the world. Then came the call for the athletes to assemble, and into the stadium we marched. What a thrill to experience the standing ovation of cheering spectators as we marched around the field.

Meg Christian sang the Gay Games anthem, "Reach for the Sky," author Rita Mae Brown acted as M.C., Metropolitan Community Churches' founder Rev. Troy Perry gave the invocation, and two former Olympians--Susan McGrievy and George Frenn--lit the traditional flame plinth.

I still shudder with excitement when I hear the triumphal theme from "Chariots of Fire." I also thrill to the recollection of the Closing Ceremonies, when Tina Turner, in spike heels and a short gold lamé dress, belted out her tunes while we danced on the field. The tradition of the Gay Games had begun.

The idea of the Gay Games was born as a dream in the mind of Dr. Tom Waddell, a physician and outstanding athlete, who had competed in the decathlon at the 1968 Olympics in Mexico City. In 1980, he began to make his dream a reality. He gathered together a group of like-minded people in San Francisco, who set up the non-profit San Francisco Arts and Athletics,

Gay Games at a Glance

Gay Games I: San Francisco, Calif.
August 28 to September 5, 1982
1,300 athletes from 179 cities

Gay Games II: San Francisco, Calif.
August 9 to 17, 1986
3,482 athletes from 259 cities

Gay Games III: Vancouver, British Columbia, Canada
August 4 to 11, 1990
more than 5,500 athletes anticipated

which was incorporated on Nov. 4, 1981, to develop and promote the idea of the games.

He had several philosophical reasons for wanting to organize the Gay Games. "The most important thing about the Games is the destruction of 'isms' like agism, sexism, and racism," he declared. "The second most important thing is the recreational aspect of competition. That's a major departure from the traditional Olympic Games....there the emphasis has always been on winning. We like to win, too, but winning in the Gay Games means self-fulfillment".

He also saw this as an opportunity to bring together a divided gay and lesbian community. "Look around at the divisiveness in the Gay community," Waddell said at the time. "The men and women don't talk to each other; a lot of the political, religious, and social groups don't talk to each other....So we got to thinking. 'What's going to bring them all together?' And we came up with the idea of sport....If people aren't into exercise and competition, most people are at least into spectating." Recognizing that the media presented the gay/lesbian community in the stereotypical roles of drag and leather, Tom also wanted the faces of lesbian and gay athletes to represent our community.

As the idea of a gay sports event began to catch on, an organizing committee was set up to carry out the logistics involved--publicity, fundraising, housing, registration, Opening and Closing Ceremonies, officiating, security, transportation, and communications. Gay Games I was overseen by San Francisco Arts and Athletics 15-member board of directors, with Tom Waddell as president and chairperson of the organizing committee.

Gay Games Facts--Softball Winners

Gay Games I

Men
Gold: San Francisco
Silver: Seattle
Bronze: Los Angeles

Women
Gold: San Francisco
Silver: San Rafael, Ca.
Bronze: Detroit

Gay Games II

Men
Gold: San Francisco
Silver: Boston
Bronze: Seattle

Women
Gold: San Francisco
Silver: Guerneville, Ca.
Bronze: Redwood City, Ca.

Gay Games Facts--Volleyball Winners

Gay Games I

Men	**Women**
Gold: Seattle	Gold: Sacramento
Silver: Los Angeles	Silver: San Francisco
Bronze: San Diego	Bronze: Not awarded

Gay Games II

Men, "A" Division	**Women**
Gold: Miami	Gold: Vancouver
Silver: Seattle	Silver: Berkeley, Ca.
Bronze: Los Angeles	Bronze: Seattle
Men ,"B" Division	
Gold: Toronto	
Silver: San Diego	
Bronze: Seattle	

Tom had great skill at infusing others with his ideas and making them want to be a part of his dream. Old friends, new acquaintances, lovers, business people, media contacts, family--all became part of Gay Games I. Through their work and Tom's inspiration, the basic principles of the Gay Games were developed:

- Equal participation by women and men
- Emphasis on participation over competition
- Emphasis upon personal best
- Inclusive versus exclusive

But these lofty ideals were not universally supported, especially not by the United States Olympic Committee. On Aug. 9, 1982, three weeks before the Games were to begin, the U.S. Olympic Committee filed suit in federal court to prevent the use of the word "olympic" in connection with the Gay Games, which had originally been billed as the "Gay Olympic Games." The "O" word had to be removed from all the Gay Games products and printed materials.

Mary Dunlap, the San Francisco Arts and Athletics attorney, argued that trying to prohibit non-commercial use of an ancient word was clearly a homophobic attempt by the U.S. Olympic Committee to violate First Amendment guarantees of free speech and association. After a series of appeals, the case went to the Supreme Court of the United States, which in June 1987, ruled in favor of the U.S. Olympic Committee, saying that, according to the Amateur Sports Act of 1978, they owned the word "olympics" and could prevent its use by other groups.

Meanwhile, Gay Games I was held and a new gay/lesbian tradition was born. On Aug. 28, 1982, more than 1,300 athletes from 12 countries, 27 states, and 179 cities paraded into San Francisco's Kezar Stadium before 8,000 spectators for the Opening Ceremonies of Gay Games I. Gay Games I was a great success. (For a listing of events and winners, see "Gay Games I," page 20.)

And then the world waited for an announcement as to the future of the Games. Vancouver was already considering being the host city. In fact, the first time I met Tom Waddell in the bustling Castro St. offices of S.F.A.A., it was to discuss Vancouver's chances. He was a tall, ruggedly handsome, serious individual. He informed me that if Vancouver intended to bid for a future Gay Games, we must consider two major issues--support of the city government and cooperation with the city police. I was confident of Vancouver's public record.

After Gay Games I, Vancouver's gay/lesbian sports community began to establish a record of experience and organizational expertise by hosting the Gay and Lesbian Summer Games from 1983 to 1985. Each year, we invited Tom Waddell to be our special guest and banquet speaker. Many late evenings were spent discussing the philosophies and the future of the Games. Tom always envisioned that they would become truly international, and he was very supportive of Vancouver as a future host city.

But in 1983 he decided that the Games would once again be held in San Francisco in order to refine the principles and practices before moving them to another city or country. He sought out former board members and future committee heads to ensure success. If approached with an idea, he

Gay Games Facts--Basketball

Gay Games I

Men	Women
Gold: San Francisco	Gold: Berkeley, Ca.
Silver: Boston	Silver: San Francisco
Bronze: Los Angeles	Bronze: Not awarded

Gay Games II

Men	Women
Gold: San Diego	Gold: San Francisco
Silver: San Francisco	Silver: Los Angeles
Bronze: Los Angeles	Bronze: Denver

would listen politely, then proclaim, "Good idea. You're in charge." Under the capable direction of Shawn Kelly as executive director, the committee structure took shape, and a core of volunteers took over the major responsibilities of sports co-chairs, registration, publicity, fundraising, and the Ceremonies.

I chose t obe a full-time volunteer in San Francisco during the summer of 1986. Each day the Gay Games office was humming with activity as we stuffed envelopes, posted mail, sold tickets, and answered questions on the telephone. What excitement when the athletes began to arrive from Sydney, New York City, Wellington, Paris, Toronto, and other places around the world. Castro St. was awash with colorful team jackets proudly proclaiming their city team names. It was reminiscent of pre-AIDS days, when lots of healthy, attractive young women and men were bustling through the shops, restaurants, and bars.

Gay Games II was held in San Francisco, from August 9 to 17, 1986. Attendance was definitely up; 3,482 men and women athletes from 259 cities competed in 17 sports. (For listing, see "Gay Games II ," page 31.) Gay Games II was the largest international sports event held in North America that year. The Games II also added a cultural component, "Procession of the Arts," featuring dance, theater, fine arts exhibits, and concerts.

Meanwhile, Vancouver had been working steadily on their bid proposal since the spring of 1985, and the committee flew down in July 1986 to make the presentation to the board of S.F.A.A. The board accepted the bid unanimously. For the 1990 site of Gay Games III, Vancouver had been chosen.

At the Closing Ceremonies of Gay Games II, what a personal thrill it was to accept the Gay Games flag from Tom and then speak to the estimated 17,000 spectators. We had come prepared with a huge Canadian Flag and a 60-foot banner proclaiming: "Vancouver, Canada--Celebration '90." We also stuck a maple leaf patch onto every athlete's identification badge with a personal invitation to "See you in Vancouver in 1990!"

I left Vancouver a week after the Closing Ceremonies and kept in telephone contact with Tom until his death in July 1987. (See Biography of Tom Waddell on page 12.)

A private memorial reception was held at his home followed by a public memorial in the rotunda of San Francisco's City Hall. Dr. Tom Waddell was remembered as an athlete, a physician, a gay activist, a visionary, and a dreamer. The event was a fitting tribute to this man whose legacy of great ideas and inspired philosophy lives on in the minds and hearts of gays and lesbians internationally.

From inspiration comes ideas. From ideas come action. From action comes inspiration. That is Tom's legacy to us and our memorial to him.

Photo: Scott McLennan

"Papa Games"

Tom Waddell

1937-1987

Dr. Thomas F. Waddell for the 49 years of his life was a champion. He was a champion in athletics; he was a champion in the cause of human rights; he was a champion in the cause of gay/lesbian rights.

Tom Waddell loved people and people loved him. His friends, lovers, associates, and admirers described him with superlatives: "a man of deep conviction," "a person who exuded warmth," "a great leader." His many roles included doctor, Olympian, lover, father, and role model for other gay people. Until his death from AIDS, he was one of the foremost leaders in the San Francisco gay/lesbian community. He served on the local board of the American Civil Liberties Union. His Mission District home, a former auditorium and athletic hall, was always open to the gay/lesbian community, and often the site of gatherings ranging from piano concerts to political fundraisers. But Tom Waddell will be best remembered as the founder of the Gay Games.

He was born Thomas Flubacher in Patterson, N.J., in 1937. His father, a bus driver, and his mother, a delicatessen operator, broke up their marriage when Tom was entering his teenage years. At first, he lived with his father. Then, at the age of 15, he moved in with Hazel and Gene Waddell, for whom he had been doing chores and with whom he was developing a family-type relationship. Six years later, they legally adopted him.

Tom Waddell suspected his homosexual orientation when he was in high school during the 1950s, a very conservative, sexually uptight time in American history. "I liked who I was. I liked what I felt," he said in a 1987 interview for *Sports Illustrated.* "But I didn't want to be this....social and physical outcast....I wanted to have lots of friends, and I realized the way I was going to do that was...through an athletic capacity, and that came easily to me."

Both of his adoptive parents were athletes and acrobats. Gene taught Tom gymnastics, and Hazel taught him dance. In fact, he considered becoming a dancer and even studied ballet briefly in New York City. But he was very uncomfortable with the "faggot dancer" stereotype so typical of the 1950s, and instead he turned his physical attention to sports.

Through his athletic ability, he earned a scholarship to Springfield College in Massachusetts and planned to become a coach. But a tragic death altered those plans. His college roommate and best friend was a premed student named Don Marshman. They were both champions on the flying rings, co-captains of the college gymnastics team, and all was going well until one afternoon when they were working out together in the gym.

While practicing swings on the rings, Marshman lost his grip, fell head-first onto the floor, and moments later died of his injuries in Waddell's arms. After recovering from the shock of this loss, Waddell decided to pursue the career Marshman had been headed toward and switched from coaching to premed. He went on to attend New Jersey College of Medicine, graduating with an M.D. in 1965.

But prior to becoming a doctor, Waddell fell in love. This happened after he graduated from Springfield College in 1959. He was working that summer at a camp in the Berkshires when he met Friedrich Engels Menaker, who operated a nearby camp for adults called the Farm. Waddell had had casual sexual encounters with men while in college, but this was his first real love. Menaker, then 63, was a major influence on Waddell. An intellectual and a radical, he transformed the thinking of Waddell, who had arrived in the Berkshires a "conservative Republican jock". Menaker and Waddell remained great friends until Menaker's death at age 90.

Also before entering medical school, Waddell tried out for, but did not make, the 1960 Olympic team as a decathlete. His next chance was not to come for another eight years.

Meanwhile, Waddell was drafted into the Army and even volunteered for paratroop duty, gritting his teeth and jumping out of planes. But when orders came for him to go to Vietnam, he refused. He was morally opposed to the war and felt he had to take this stand. He feared his refusal would lead to a court martial and prison term, but, instead, the Army transferred him to Walter Reed Army Medical Center. At the Washington, D.C., facility, he studied tropical medicine. Then in 1968, he petitioned the Army for a transfer to Los Angeles to try out for the 1968 Olympics. Permission was granted, and this time he made the team.

At the 1968 Olympic Games in Mexico City, he competed in the decathlon. Although he won no medals, he placed sixth, broke five personal records, achieved a total of 7,720 points, and became one of the all-time top 10 American decathletes up to that time.

The year 1968 was the beginning of great cultural and social change in America. The student movement, protests against the Vietnam war, the black civil rights movement were all underway. In a controversial gesture, medal-winning black U.S. Olympians gave the clenched-fist Black Power salute as the national anthem was played, and Waddell identified with the feelings of these black athletes. He believed deeply in the struggle against all injustice--agism, racism, and sexism. And after the 1968 Olympic experience, he apparently began to dream of a sports event that would showcase gay/lesbian ability and pride.

Before he began to act on his dream, he set off on a successful medical career, working from 1974 to 1981 as medical director of the Wittaker Corporation, a job that frequently took him to the Middle East. Then he became chief physician at a San Francisco public health clinic.

But in 1980 he began taking steps to make the Gay Games a reality. He set about forming the organization that in November 1981 legally became the non-profit San Francisco Arts and Athletics, Inc. He was the first president. In August 1982, SFAA sponsored what it had planned to call the "Gay Olympic Games."

Three weeks before the games were to begin, the United States Olympic Committee filed suit to prevent use of the generic word "olympics" in connection with the Gay Games. Waddell and the SFAA fought back, eventually taking the case all the way to the U.S. Supreme Court. This was one competition, however, that he was destined not to win. In 1987, the Supreme Court ruled that the Olympic Committee owned the word "olympics" and could control its use. (See History of the Gay Games.)

Tom Waddell was a man who wanted to experience life in all its richness--and that included parenthood. His opportunity came around the same time that he was "fathering" Gay Games I. Sara Lewinstein, a lesbian activist and athlete, SFAA board member, and close friend, popped the question: "How would you like to have a baby with me?" Tears came to his eyes, he reportedly recalled, and after Gay Games I was over, he and Lewinstein went away together to conceive a child. Their daughter, Jessica, was born in August 1983. Waddell and Lewinstein married. Each, however, lived in their own respective homes. Jessica alternated spending time at each household.

It was shortly before Gay Games II was scheduled to begin in August 1986 that Waddell developed *pneumocystis carinii pneumonia*, the type of pneumonia so common in AIDS. Two weeks later, his lover was also diagnosed with AIDS. Drugs cleared up the pneumocystis temporarily, and Waddell went on to compete in Gay Games II, winning a gold medal in the javelin throw.

But he had no illusions about what lay ahead. "I look at the statistics," he said, "I look at what that means, and I can freak out, which isn't going to do me any good at all, or I can say this is what *is*."

He admitted to moments in the night when he would think about not seeing the future unfold, not seeing his daughter grow up, and he would cry. He considered crying to be healthy and cleansing for himself and for anyone. "And then," he said, "you have to say, O.K., now let's get on with what I think is real. And what is real is that there are still things to be said, things to be done."

One of the things he did before he died was appear on the ABC national news feature program, *20/20*, to tell the story of his remarkable life, his story as a gay man.

On July 7, 1987, after putting his personal and financial affairs in order, he stopped taking all medication. About two days later, he slipped into a coma. His final words before he lost consciousness were: "Well, this should be interesting." He died in his home on July 11.

Hundreds of people gathered on July 18 in San Francisco's City Hall to celebrate the life of Tom Waddell. The dignitaries included the city's health commissioner and the mayor, Dianne Feinstein. Also present was Barry McDell of the Metropolitan Vancouver Athletics and Arts Association, chosen to sponsor the 1990 Gay Games III.

In his remarks McDell made this pledge, "The dream will live on, I promise."

Photo: Scott McLennan

Profile of

GAY GAMES I

August 28 to September 5, 1982
San Francisco, Calif.
Sponsored by San Francisco Arts & Athletics, Inc.

Gay Games Anthem:
"Reach for the Sky," by George McMahon and Brian Bliss

Opening Day Ceremonies: Kezar Stadium

M.C.: Rita Mae Brown
Invocation: Rev. Troy D. Perry
Entertainment:
Foggy City Squares; San Francisco Gay Freedom Day Marching Band and Twirling Corps;Gay Games Flag Corps; Great American Yankee Freedom Band, Los Angeles;Sistah Boom; Meg Christian
Special Guest Star: Tina Turner

Athletic Events

Basketball
Bowling
Cycling
Marathon
Soccer
Powerlifting
Diving
Track & Field
Wrestling

Billiards
Boxing
Golf
Physique
Softball
Swimming
Tennis
Volleyball

Closing Day Ceremonies: Kezar Stadium

M.C.: Armistead Maupin
Entertainment: San Francisco Gay Freedom Day Marching Band and Twirling Corps; Gay Games Flag Corps; 800 Voice Chorus
Guest Speaker: Congressman Phillip Burton
Special Guest Star: Stephanie Mills

Countries, States, and Cities Represented by the Gay Games I Athletes

AUSTRALIA
Artarmon
Brisbane
North Sydney
Sydney
BELGIUM
Brussels
CANADA
Burnaby
Edmonton
Montreal
Pitt Meadows
Surrey
Vancouver
Windsor
ENGLAND
Birmingham
FRANCE
Riquewihar
IRELAND
Dublin
ISRAEL
Tel Aviv
NEW ZEALAND
Auckland
Christchurch
WEST GERMANY
Essen

UNITED STATES
ARIZONA
Green Valley
Phoenix
Tucson
CALIFORNIA
Alameda
Albany
Aptos
Atherton
Bella Vista
Belmont
Berkeley
Beverly Hills
Capitola
Cardiff
Carmichael
Cathedral City
Concord
Corte Madera
Cupertino
Daly City
Davis
Downey
East Palo Alto
El Cerrito
El Sobrante
Foster City
Fremont
Fresno
Glendale
Goleta
Guerneville
Hayward
Healdsburg
Honeydew
Huntington Beach
Kensington
Long Beach
Los Altos
Los Angeles
Martinez
Menlo Park
Mill Valley
Millbrae
Modesto
Mountain View
Mt. Washington
Napa
National City
Nipoma
Novato
Oakland
Palo Alto
Pittsburgh
Pleasanton
Redondo Beach
Redwood City
Richmond
Rio Nido
Sacramento
San Anselmo
San Bruno
San Diego
San Francisco
San Jose
San Leandro
San Lorenzo
San Mateo
San Rafael
Santa Clara
Santa Cruz

Santa Rosa
Sherman Oaks
Soquel
Stanford
Sunnyvale
Ventura
Walnut Creek
Woodside
COLORADO
Boulder
Denver
Lafayette
Woodridge
DISTRICT OF COLUMBIA
Washington
DELAWARE
Wilmington
FLORIDA
Coconut Grove
Fort Lauderdale
Hollywood
Lauderdale Lakes
Miami Shores
North Miami
GEORGIA
Atlanta
HAWAII
Honolulu
ILLINOIS
Blue Island
Chicago
INDIANA
Indianapolis
KENTUCKY
Louisville
MASSACHUSETTS
Boston
Brighton
Brookline
Burlington
Cambridge
Dorchester
Hyde Park
Lynn
Malden
Medford
Quincy
Roslindale
Somerville
Wakefield
Winthrop
MARYLAND
Baltimore
MICHIGAN
Albion
Canton
Detroit
East Detroit
Ferndale
Kalamazoo
Madison Heights
Mt. Clemens
Royal Oaks
Southfield
St. Clair Shores
Sterling Heights
Wyandotte
MINNESOTA
Bloomington
Edina
Hopkins
Minneapolis
Minnetonka
Richfield
St. Paul
MISSOURI
Kansas City
St. Louis
NORTH CAROLINA
Reidsville
NEW YORK STATE
Astoria
Ballston Spa
New York City
Rochester
OHIO
Cleveland Heights
Columbus
OREGON
Eugene
Portland
TEXAS
Houston
San Antonio
UTAH
Salt Lake City
VIRGINIA
Alexandria
Arlington
Virginia Beach
WASHINGTON STATE
Bellevue
Bothell
Kent
Kirkland
Maple Valley
Mercier Island
Seattle
Vancouver
WISCONSIN
Greendale
Madison
Milwaukee
WYOMING
Cheyenne

GAY GAMES I

Individual and Team Athletic Events

In individual competitions, the time or distance of only the Gold Medal winners is given. Names are not given, because for personal or professional reasons some individuals may not want their association with the Gay Games made public at this time. Distances are in meters unless otherwise specified.

TRACK & FIELD

Hammer Throw	59.58
Discus	
Women	33.48
Men	36.34
100 Meters	
Women	12.7
Men	11.2
200 Meters	
Women	26.4
Men	23.1
400 Meters	
Women	59.7
Men	51.0
800 Meters	
Women	2.19.0
Men	1.59.1
1500 Meters	
Women	5.06.1
Men	4.06.2
5000Meters	
Women	18.25.7
Men	15.34.2
10,000 Meters	
Women	36.05.2
Men	NA
100 Meter Hurdles	
Women	16.4
Men	16.4
400 Meter Relay	
Mixed	46.9
1600 Meter Relay	
Mixed	3.51.1
Shot Put	
Women	10.44
Men	10.05
Long Jump	
Women	16' 11.5"
Men	19'0.5"
High Jump	
Women	4'4"
Men	5'10"
Javelin	
Women	94' 5"
Men	173' 8"
Marathon	
Women	
Under 40	3.23.20
Men	
Under 40	2.30.41

Marathon	
Women	
Over 40	3.59.49
Men	
Over 40	3.09.27

Pentathlon	Points
Women	2286
Men	None
Decathlon	
Women	None
Men	4559

S W I M M I N G

50 Yard Backstroke--Women	
Under 25	36.62
26 to 35	35.46

50 Yard Backstroke-- Men	
Under 25	28.10
26 to 35	29.02
36 to 45	29.01
46 and over	42.30

100 Yard Backstroke--Women	
Under 25	1.18.85
26 to 35	1.32.21
36 to 45	2.17.49

100 Yard Backstroke--Men	
Under 25	1.01.35
26 to 35	1.02.89
36 to 45	1.08.38

200 Yard Backstroke--Women	
Under 25	2.27.67
26 to 35	3.04.99

200 Yard Backstroke--Men	
Under 25	2.18.23
26 to 35	2.30.25
36 to 45	2.30.25

50 Yard Butterfly--Women	
Under 25	28.82
26 to 35	29.32

50 Yard Butterfly--Men	
Under 25	24.84
26 to 35	25.70
36 to 45	26.82
46 and over	N. T.

100 Yard Butterfly--Women	
Under 25	1.05.66
26 to 35	1.15.56

100 Yard Butterfly--Men	
Under 25	54.68
26 to 25	58.33
36 to 45	1.42.48

200 Yard Butterfly--Women	
Under 25	2.45.58
26 to 35	2.31.22

200 Yard Butterfly--Men	
Under 25	2.40.67
26 to 35	2.26.06
36 to 45	3.46.88

50 Yard Breaststroke--Women	
Under 25	37.80
26 to 35	36.23
36 to 45	45.52

50 Yard Breaststroke--Men	
Under 25	29.54
26 to 35	31.15
36 to 45	42.24
46 and over	55.96

100 Yard Breaststroke--Women	
Under 25	1.22.98
26 to 35	1.17.29
36 to 45	2.21.06

100 Yard Breaststroke--Men	
Under 25	1.00.70
26 to 35	1.09.45
36 to 45	1.27.10
200 Yard Breaststroke--Women	
Under 25	3.03.23
26 to 35	2.46.81
200 Yard Breaststroke--Men	
Under 25	2.15.40
26 to 35	2.32.44
36 to 45	3.12.48
50 Yard Freestyle--Women	
Under 25	25.46
26 to 35	26.73
36 to 45	36.93
50 Yard Freestyle--Men	
Under 25	24.32
26 to 35	22.74
36 to 45	24.18
46 and over	33.15
100 Yard Freestyle--Women	
Under 25	56.22
26 to 35	59.63
100 Yard Freestyle--Men	
Under 25	52.51
26 to 35	52.08
36 to 45	1.02.73
46 and over	1.21.19
200 Yard Freestyle--Women	
Under 25	2.14.38
26 to 35	2.18.42
200 Yard Freestyle--Men	
Under 25	1.56.14
26 to 35	1.55.82
36 to 45	2.07.29
400 Yard Freestyle--Women	
Under 25	5.12.19
26 to 35	5.02.41
36 to 45	7.52.00
400 Yard Freestyle--Men	
Under 25	4.18.31
26 to 35	4.16.34
36 to 45	5.46.78
800 Yard Freestyle--Women	
Under 25	10.43.32
26 to 35	11.28.68
36 to 45	16.10.73
800 Yard Freestyle--Men	
Under 25	9.16.77
26 to 35	9.00.61
36 to 45	12.02.42
1,650 Yard Freestyle	
Women	22.37.16
Men	19.04.71
100 Yard Medley Relay--Women	
San Francisco	1.08.03
100 Yard Medley Relay--Men	
Los Angeles	49.00
100 Yard Medley Relay--Mixed	
New York	59.67
200 Yard Medley Relay--Women	
Berkeley	2.09.92
200 Yard Medley Relay--Men	
Los Angeles	1.45.79
400 Yard Medley Relay--Men	
Los Angeles	3.57.77
100 Yard Freestyle Relay--Mixed	
Kentfield	52.22
200 Yard Freestyle Relay--Women	
San Francisco	1.52.04
200 Yard Freestyle Relay--Men	
Los Angeles	1.35.95
200 Yard Freestyle Relay--Mixed	
San Francisco	1.39.47

400 Yard Freestyle Relay--Mixed

Berkeley	4.40.41

100 Yd. Individ. Medley--Women

Under 25	1.04.29
26 to 35	1.14.37

100 Yd. Individ. Medley--Men

Under 25	57.20
26 to 35	59.14
36 to 45	1.04.32
46 and over	1.39.67

200 Yd. Individ. Medley--Women

Under 25	2.31.22
26 to 35	2.27.91

200 Yd. Individ. Medley--Men

Under 25	2.06.71
26 to 35	2.17.08
36 to 45	2.23.67

BILLIARDS

Women's Team 8 Ball

1st	San Francisco
2nd	Daly City, Ca
3rd	Boston, Mass.

Men's Team 8 Ball

1st	San Francisco
2nd	Minneapolis
3rd	Vancouver

Mixed 8 Ball

1st	San Francisco

Women's Team 9 Ball

1st	San Francisco
2nd	Boston, Mass

Men's Team 9 Ball

1st	San Francisco
2nd	Los Angeles
3rd	Pleasant Hill, Ca

Mixed 9 Ball

1st	San Francisco
2nd	Los Angeles

Individual Billiards Competition:

Women's 8 Ball
Men's 8 Ball

Women's 9 Ball
Men's 9 Ball

BASKETBALL

Women

1st	Berkeley
2nd	San Francisco

Men

1st	San Francisco
2nd	Boston, Mass.
3rd	Los Angeles

VOLLEYBALL

Women

1st	Sacramento
2nd	San Francisco

Men

1st	Seattle
2nd	Los Angeles
3rd	San Diego

TENNIS

Women's Doubles	
1st	Berkeley
2nd	San Francisco
3rd	Sacramento

Men's Doubles	
1st	Sydney, Australia
2nd	Menlo Park, Ca.
3rd	Detroit, Mich.

Mixed Doubles	
1st	San Francisco
2nd	Berkeley
3rd	San Francisco

Other Tennis Competition
- Women's Singles
- Men's Singles

BOWLING

Women's Team Points

1st	San Francisco	4846
2nd	Napa, Ca.	4744
3rd	Sacramento	4315

Men's Team Points

1st	San Rafael, Ca.	4264
2nd	Seattle	4091
3rd	Denver	4065

Other Bowling Competition
- Women Individual
- Men Individual

POWERLIFTING

Women 52 kg.	560 lb.
Women 56 kg	465 lb.
Women 60 kg.	760 lb.
Women 67.5 kg.	550 lb.
Women 75 kg.	725 lb.
Women 82.5 kg.	615 lb.

Men 60 kg.	595 lb.
Men 100 kg.	1,255 lb.
Men 110-125 kg.	1,810 lb.

SOFTBALL

Women	
1st	San Francisco
2nd	San Rafael
3rd	Detroit

Men	
1st	San Francisco
2nd	Seattle
3rd	Los Angeles

GOLF

Gross Scores--Women	
1st	296
2nd	300
3rd	315

Gross Scores--Men	
1st	234
2nd	281
3rd	312

Net Scores--Women	
1st	212
2nd	213
3rd	215

Net Scores--Men	
1st	212
2nd	213
3rd	218

OTHER COMPETITIONS

Wrestling

114.5 lbs.
125.5 lbs.
136.5 lbs.
149.5 lbs.
163.0 lbs.
180.5 lbs.
198.0 lbs.
220.0 lbs.

Physique

Women	Lightweight
Women	Heavyweight
Men	Lightweight
Men	Middleweight
Men	Light Heavyweight
Men	Heavyweight

Diving

Men Under 25
Men Over 25

Boxing

Women	Bantamweight
Women	Featherweight
Women	Lightweight
Women	Light Welterweight
Women	Welterweight
Men	Lightweight
Men	Welterweight

Cycling

Cyclo-Cross
- Women
- Men

Road Race
- Women
- Men

Soccer

Although this was a scheduled competitive event in Gay Games I, no scores are available

Photo: Scott McLennan

Profile of

GAY GAMES II

August 9 to August 17, 1986
San Francisco, California

Sponsored by San Francisco Arts & Athletics, Inc.

Gay Games Anthem:
"Reach for the Sky," by George McMahon and Brian Bliss

Opening Day Ceremonies: Kezar Stadium

Host: Scott Beach

MC: Rita Mae Brown

Entertainment: Gwenn Avery & Against All Odds Band; Vocal Minority; Barbary Coast Cloggers; Napata Mero; The Saddletramps; The San Jose Spurs; The Savoy Stompers; Joe Poltrone; Sharon McNight; Lesbian & Gay Band of America; Golden Gate Precision Dancers

Presentation of Colors: Alexander Hamilton Post #448 of the American Legion

Invocation: Rev. Jane A. Spahr

Athletic Events

Basketball
Bowling
Cycling
Marathon
Soccer
Powerlifting
Tennis
Volleyball
Racquetball
Billiards/Pool
Triathlon
Golf
Physique
Softball
Swimming & Diving
Track & Field
Wrestling

Closing Day Ceremonies: Kezar Stadium

Host: Scott Beach

M.C.: Armistead Maupin

Entertainment: The Hayward Raw Rahs; Samantha Samuels; Greater Bay Area Square Dancers; Golden Gate Precision Dancers; The Greater Bay Area Choruses; Lesbian & Gay Marching Band of America

Closing Address: Dr. Tom Waddell

Special Guest Star: Jennifer Holliday

Countries, States, and Cities Represented by the Gay Games II Athletes

AUSTRALIA
Adelaide
Blacktown
Bondi Beach
Brisbane
Jabiru
Melbourne
North Sydney
Paddington
Sydney
BRAZIL
Rio de Janeiro
CANADA
Acadie
Calgary
Collingwood
Edmonton
Montreal
North York
Ottawa
Quebec
Scarborough
Surrey
Toronto
Vancouver
West Vancouver
Winnipeg
ENGLAND
London
Manchester
Shalfor-Surrey

FRANCE
Courbevoie
Dunkerque
Paris
GREECE
Athens
GUAM
Guam
IRELAND
Dublin
ISRAEL
Tel Aviv
ITALY
Florence
Rome
JAPAN
Tokyo
MEXICO
Mexico City
THE NETHERLANDS
Haarlem
NICARAGUA
Managua
NEW ZEALAND
Auckland
Christchurch
Rotorua
Wellington
SAMOA
Pago Pago
VIRGIN ISLANDS
St. Croix

WEST GERMANY
Ahrweiler

UNITED STATES
ALABAMA
Birmingham
Mobile
Montgomery
ARIZONA
Glendale
Phoenix
Tempe
Tucson
CALIFORNIA
Alameda
Albany
Aptos
Arcata
Avila Beach
Bakersfield
Benicia
Berkeley
Burlingame
Burbank
Campbell
Castro Valley
Cazadero
Chico
Chino
Cloverdale
Concord
Cupertino

Daly City
Danville
El Cajon
El Cerrito
Emeryville
Fly Creek
Forestville
Foster City
Fremont
Fresno
Froggy Acres
Garden Grove
Gardena
Granada Hills
Guerneville
Half Moon Bay
Hayward
Hillsborough
Huntington Beach
Irvine
Laguna Beach
Lagunitas
Lafayette
Long Beach
Los Altos Hills
Los Angeles
Los Gatos
Martinez
Menlo Park
Mill Valley
Modesto
Moss Beach
Mountain View
Newport Beach
Nicasio
Oakland
Pacifica
Palo Alto
Paradise
Pasadena
Pebble Beach
Petaluma
Piedmont
Pleasant Hill
Pleasonton
Point Richmond
Redondo Beach
Redwood City
Rialto
Richmond
Riverside
Sacramento
San Bruno
San Carlos
San Diego
San Francisco
San Jose
San Leandro
San Luis Obispo
San Mateo
San Pablo
Santa Barbara
Santa Clara
Santa Cruz
Santa Monica
Santa Rosa
Sausalito
Sonoma
South San Francisco
Torrance
Turlock
Ukiah
Vallejo
Ventura
Walnut Creek
West Hollywood
West Los Angeles
Woodside

COLORADO

Arvada
Aurora
Colorado Springs
Denver
Durango
Fort Collins
Littleton
Wheat Ridge

CONNECTICUT

Norwalk

DISTRICT OF COLUMBIA

Washington

FLORIDA

Fort Lauderdale
Key West
Miami

GEORGIA

Atlanta
Doraville

HAWAII

Honolulu
Kailua
Lahaina

IOWA

Des Moines
Iowa City

ILLINOIS

Chicago
Springfield

INDIANA

French Lick
Indianapolis
Jeffersonville
Sheridan

KANSAS

Kansas City

KENTUCKY

Lexington
Louisville

LOUISIANA
New Orleans
MASSACHUSETTS
Amherst
Belchertown
Boston
Cambridge
Provincetown
MARYLAND
Baltimore
MICHIGAN
Canton
Detroit
East Lansing
Flint
Traverse City
MINNESOTA
Minneapolis
St. Paul
MISSOURI
Kansas City
St. Louis
MONTANA
Laurel
Utica
Valier
NORTH CAROLINA
Greensboro
Lumberton
NEBRASKA
Harrison
Lincoln
Omaha
NEW JERSEY
Bogota
East Rutherford
Wayne
West New York
NEW MEXICO
Albuquerque
Corrales
Taos
NEVADA
Reno
NEW YORK STATE
Brooklyn
Fly Creek
Hawthorne
Hyde Park
New York City
Rochester
Wading Creek
OHIO
Cincinnati
Cleveland
Cleveland Heights
Columbus
Dayton
Elyria
Shaker Heights
OKLAHOMA
Norman
OREGON
Eugene
Portland
PENNSYLVANIA
McKees Rocks
Philadelphia
Pittsburgh
SOUTH CAROLINA
Greenville
Summerville
Sumter
TENNESSEE
Hixson
Memphis
TEXAS
Austin
Bellaire
Corpus Christi
Dallas
Fort Worth
Galveston
Houston
San Antonio
West University
UTAH
Salt Lake City
VIRGINIA
Alexandria
Arlington
Norfolk
Portsmouth
VERMONT
Hinesburg
Middlebury
WASHINGTON STATE
Seattle
Tukwila
WISCONSIN
Greendale
Madison
Milwaukee
WEST VIRGINIA
Chapmanville

GAY GAMES II

Individual and Team Athletic Events

In individual competitions, the time or distance of only the Gold Medal winner is given. Names are not given, because for personal or professional reasons some individuals may not wish to be associated with the Gay Games at this time. Most events are grouped by sex and age. Distance is presumed to be in meters if feet and inches are not indicated.

TRACK & FIELD

100 Meters--Women	
18 to 29	:14.38
30 to 34	:14.57
200 Meters--Women	
18 to 29	:27.81
30 to 34	:27.79
40 to 44	:37.98
400 Meters--Women	
18 to 29	:57.56
30 to 34	1:04.59
35 to 39	1:12.24
40 to 44	1:24.51
800 Meters--Women	
18 to 29	2:14.32
30 to 34	2:31.26
35 to 39	2:50.85
40 to 44	3:07.84
1.500 Meters--Women	
18 to 29	5:46.12
30 to 34	5:18.10
35 to 39	6:43.41
40 to 44	6:53.85
45 to 49	6:19.46
5,000 Meters--Women	
18 to 29	17:46.60
30 to 34	20:57.00
35 to 39	18.30.30
40 to 44	21:26.10
45 to 49	23.15:00
10,000 Meters--Women	
18 to 29	36:48:60
30 to 34	42:10.50
35 to 39	37.47.40
40 to 44	46:33.70
45 to 49	46:30.50
100 Meter Hurdles--Women	
18 to 29	:19.69
4 X 100 Meter Relay--	
Women, 18 to 29	
Los Angeles	:50.76
Women, 30 to 39	
New York	1:09.80
4 X 400 Meter Relay--	
Women, 18 to 29	
Los Angeles	4:11.10
Long Jump--Women	
18 to 29	16'10.25"
30 to 34	11'09.25"
Shot Put--Women	
18 to 29	41'07.50"
30 to 34	27'02.25"
40 to 44	27'05.00"
45 to 49	28'00.00"
Discus--Women	
18 to 29	127'09.00"
30 to 34	66'03.00"
40 to 44	67'05.00"
45 to 49	81'02.00"

High Jump--Women

18 to 29	5'05"

Javelin--Women

18 to 29	136'06"
30 to 34	78'03"
40 to 44	86'02"
45 to 49	79'07"

100 Meters--Men

18 to 29	:11.49
30 to 34	:11.99
35 to 39	:11.67
40 to 44	:12.24
45 to 49	:12.60

200 Meters--Men

18 to 29	:23.19
30 to 34	:24.48
35 to 39	:24.20
40 to 44	:25.50
45 to 49	:28.40
50 and over	:31.18

400 Meters--Men

19 to 29	:53.26
30 to 34	:54.28
35 to 39	:53.03
40 to 44	:56.94
45 to 49	1:06.91

800 Meters--Men

18 to 29	2:01.81
30 to 34	2:09.84
35 to 39	2:13.28
40 to 44	2:27.69
50 and over	2:44.43

1,500 Meters--Men

18 to 29	4:17.16
30 to 34	4:23.64
35 to 39	5:12.42
40 to 44	5:20.74
50 and over	5:20.04

5,000 Meters--Men

18 to 29	16:03.90
30 to 34	16:28.80
35 to 39	15:56.10
40 to 44	18:46.00
45 to 49	18:40.70
50 and over	17:57.40

10,000 Meters--Men

18 to 29	31:41.10
30 to 34	34:22.20
35 to 39	33:00.90
40 to 44	38:51.30
45 to 49	36:15.60
50 and over	38:45.10

100 Meter Hurdles--Men

18 to 29	:16.27
30 to 34	:16.55
35 to 39	:19.94
40 to 44	:18.23

4 X 100 Meter Relay

Men, 18 to 29	
San Francisco	:45.52
Men, 30 to 39	
San Francisco "A"	:45.14
Men, 40 to 49	
New York "B"	:53.90

4 X 400 Meter Relay

Men, 18 to 29	
San Francisco	3:40.80
Men, 30 to 39	
San Francisco "A"	3:46.89
Men, 40 to 49	
New York "A"	4:.21.61

Long Jump--Men

18 to 29	20'11.50"
30 to 34	20'01.50"
35 to 39	15'08.00"
40 to 44	17'09.00"

Shotput

18 to 29	31.375

30 to 34	26.325
35 to 39	25.115
40 to 44	32.1125

Discus--Men

18 to 29	43.84
35 to 39	17.18
40 to 44	31.80

High Jump--Men

18 to 29	6'11.00"
30 to 34	5'07.00"
35 to 39	6'09.00"

Javelin--Men

18 to 29	135'06.00"
35 to 39	123'04.00"
40 to 44	119'03.00"
45 to 49	104'10.00"

Hammer Throw--Men

18 to 29	90'04.00"
40 to 44	74'05.00"

4 X 200 Relay--Mixed

18 to 29, San Francisco	1:46.74
30 to 39, San Francisco	1:51.20
40 to 49, New York	2:23.93

Decathlon--Men only

Age groups:

18 to 29

20 to 34

35 to 39

TRIATHLON--Women

18 years	2.27.24
19 to 29	2:13.05
30 to 39	2:06.13
40 to 49	2:42.34

TRIATHLON--Men

19 to 29	1:48.09
30 to 39	1:52.32
40 to 49	2.21.30

SWIMMING

50 Butterfly--Women

19 to 24	:29.15
25 to 29	:28.89
30 to 34	:29.92
35 to 39	:31.28

100 Butterfly--Women

19 to 24	1:07.77
25 to 29	1:01.61
30 to 34	1:04.09

50 Freestyle--Women

19 to 24	:26.63
25 to 29	:25.31
30 to 34	:27.20
35 to 39	:27.80
40 to 44	:32.31
45 to 49	:40.44

100 Freestyle--Women

19 to 24	1:00.94
25 to 29	:55.69
30 to 34	:59.11
35 to 39	1:02.23
40 to 44	1:12.44

200 Freestyle--Women

19 to 24	2:12.64
25 to 29	1:58.11
30 to 34	2:27.53
35 to 39	2:28.79
40 to 44	2:39.91
45 to 49	3:21.97

500 Freestyle--Women

25 to 29	5:14.41
30 to 34	6:23.08
35 to 39	7:13.86
40 to 44	7:16.87
45 to 49	10:44.31

1,650 Freestyle--Women

19 to 24	20:21.94
25 to 29	20:27.84
30 to 34	21:41.44
35 to 39	24:56.31
45 to 49	38:11.44

200 Freestyle Relay:
Women Under 120 pounds

Gold: Santa Rosa, Ca.	2:01.59
Silver: Danville, Ca.	2:04.36
Bronze: Seattle	2:27.21

Women Over 120 pounds

Gold: W. Hollywood A	1:54.75
Silver: San Francisco A	1:59.20
Bronze: San Francisco B	2:45.06

400 Freestyle Relay
Women Under 120 pounds

Gold: Santa Rosa, Ca.	4:41.33

Women Over 120 pounds

Gold: Berkeley, Ca	4:29.51
Silver: San Francisco A	5:38.95

50 Backstroke--Women

19 to 24	:39.65
25 to 29	:38.15
30 to 34	:33.26
35 to 39	:37.52
40 to 44	:45.91

100 Backstroke--Women

19 to 24	1:11.22
25 to 29	1:17.47
30 to 34	1:11.55
35 to 39	1:20.52
40 to 44	1:39.89

200 Backstroke--Women

25 to 29	2:45.30
30 to 34	2:38.72
35 to 39	2:50.78
40 to 44	3:45.75

50 Breaststroke--Women

19 to 24	:34.51
25 to 29	:37.10
30 to 34	:35.89
35 to 39	:40.95
40 to 44	:46.17
45 to 49	:51.62

100 Breaststroke--Women

19 to 24	1:14.83
25 to 29	1:14.02
30 to 34	1:14.83
35 to 39	1:33.10
40 to 44	1:49.75
45 to 49	1:48.01

200 Breaststroke--Women

19 to 24	2:39.40
25 to 29	2:26.78
30 to 34	2:40.58
35 to 39	3:51.14
40 to 44	3:40.25

100 Individual Medley--Women

19 to 24	1:11.50
25 to 29	1:04.55
30 to 34	1:07.89
35 to 39	1:11.62

200 Individual Medley--Women
Results Missing

400 Individual Medley--Women

24 to 29	5:52.47
30 to 34	6:22.22

200 Medley Relay
Women Under 120 pounds

Gold: Santa Rosa, Ca.	2:22.17
Silver: Danville, Ca.	2:26.64

Women Over 120 pounds

Gold: W. Hollywood	2:07.11
Silver: Berkeley, Ca.	2:15.04
Bronze: San Francisco A	2:25.00

50 Butterfly--Men

19 to 24	:24.37
25 to 29	:23.03
30 to 34	:26.17
35 to 39	:25.48
40 to 44	:28.61
45 to 49	:31.17

100 Butterfly--Men

19 to 24	:51.40
25 to 29	:51.40
30 to 34	:56.72
35 to 39	:58.00
40 to 44	1:22.97
45 to 49	1:18.37

200 Butterfly--Men

19 to 24	1:59.52
25 to 29	2:08.93
30 to 34	2:08.93
35 to 39	2:40.14

50 Freestyle--Men

19 to 24	:21.81
25 to 29	:22.73
30 to 34	:22.61
35 to 39	:22.86
40 to 44	:24.81
45 to 49	:26.77
50 to 54	:30.99
55 to 59	:29.24
60 and over	:38.83

100 Freestyle--Men

19 to 24	:46.91
25 to 29	:48.67
30 to 34	:50.47
35 to 39	:50.42
40 to 44	:55.62
45 to 49	1:02.02
50 to 54	1:08.77
55 to 59	1:07.04
60 and over	1:29.83

200 Freestyle--Men

19 to 24	1:46.14
25 to 29	1:45.45
30 to 34	1:52.56
35 to 39	1:58.79
40 to 44	2:42.29
45 to 49	2:21.83
50 to 54	2:28.50
55 to 59	2:47.78
60 and over	3:27.31

500 Freestyle--Men

19 to 24	5:08.78
25 to 29	4:56.95
30 to 34	5:13.20
35 to 39	5:30.15
40 to 44	7:29.37
45 to 49	6:44.28
50 to 54	6:43.95
60 and over	7:28.58

1,650 Freestyle--Men

19 to 24	18:43.56
25 to 29	17:39.61
30 to 34	18:18.69
35 to 39	18:20.04
40 to 44	26:39.19
45 to 49	24:06.13
50 to 54	23:37.00
55 to 59	28:25.75

200 Freestyle Relay

Men Under 120 pounds

Gold: W. Hollywood A	1:30.54
Silver: San Francisco A	1:31.74
Bronze: Denver	1:36.15

Men Over 120 pounds

Gold: San Francisco A	1:32.42
Silver: San Diego A	1:34.17
Bronze: W. Hollywood A	1:34.59

Men Over 160 pounds

Gold: San Francisco A	1:47.99
Silver: Vancouver	1:54.01
Bronze: Australia	2:00.92

400 Freestyle Relay

Men Under 120 pounds

Gold: W. Hollywood	3:23.62

Silver: San Francisco A 3:26.61
Bronze: San Diego 3:34.72

Men Over 120 pounds
Gold: San Francisco A 3:26.72
Silver: San Diego A 3:32.06
Bronze: San Diego B 3:40.12

Men Over 160 pounds
Gold: San Francisco A 4:07.34
Silver: Vancouver 4:20.33
Bronze: Australia 4:53.10

50 Backstroke--Men

19 to 24	:26.47
25 to 29	:24.84
30 to 34	:27.06
35 to 39	:29.99
40 to 44	:31.72
45 to 49	:37.48
50 to 54	:41.67
55 to 59	:56.10
60 and over	:44.70

100 Backstroke--Men

19 to 24	:58.58
25 to 29	:54.55
30 to 34	:59.61
35 to 39	1:00.64
40 to 44	1:11.13
45 to 49	1:11.53
55 to 59	2:00.41
60 and over	1:43.15

200 Backstroke--Men

19 to 24	2:02.13
25 to 29	2:21.61
30 to 34	2:13.87
35 to 39	2:32.72
40 to 44	3:30.70
45 to 49	2:44.37
50 to 54	3:17.34
60 and over	3:42.76

50 Breaststroke--Men

19 to 24	:28.81
25 to 29	:28.81
30 to 34	:29.28
35 to 39	:31.15
40 to 44	:41.60
45 to 49	:41.67
55 to 59	1:13.02

100 Breaststroke--Men

19 to 24	1:03.94
25 to 29	1:02.61
30 to 34	1:04.51
35 to 39	1:12.40
40 to 44	1:28.19

200 Breaststroke--Men

19 to 24	2:25.61
25 to 29	2:19.00
30 to 34	2:21.92
35 to 39	2:54.09
40 to 44	3:23.55

100 Individual Medley--Men

19 to 24	:54.77
25 to 29	:57.64
30 to 34	:57.09
35 to 39	:58.64
40 to 44	1:08.73
45 to 49	1:08.78
55 to 59	1:24.46

200 Individual Medley--Men
Results Missing

400 Individual Medley--Men

19 to 24	4:15.94
25 to 29	4:19.73
30 to 34	4:36.65
35 to 39	5:36.72
45 to 49	6:05.87

200 Medley Relay
Men Under 120 pounds
Gold: W.Hollywood A 1:42.02
Silver: San FranciscoA 1:44.60
Bronze: W.Hollywood B 1:47.98

Men Over 120 pounds
Gold: San Diego A 1:46.99
Silver: San Francisco A 1:48.40
Bronze: New York A 1:49.24

Men Over 160 pounds
Gold: Vancouver 2:11.67
Silver: Berkeley, Ca. 2:19.09

200 Medley Relay
Mixed Under 120 pounds
Gold: S.F. Rec. & Park 1:54.06
Silver: San Francsico A 1:59.98
Bronze: Sacramento 2:06.75

Mixed Over 120 pounds
Gold: W.Hollywood A 1:53.39
Silver: W. Hollywood B 1:58.39
Bronze: San Francisco B 1:59.09

Mixed Over 160 pounds
Gold: Berkeley, Ca. 2:19.83
Silver: San Francisco A 2:47.93

200 Freestyle Relay
Mixed Under 120 pounds
Gold: San Francisco A 1:44.83
Silver: Seattle 1:48.20
Bronze:W.Hollywood B 1:49.21

Mixed Over 120 pounds
Gold: W.Hollywood A 1:48.91
Silver: New York 1:50.42
Bronze: San FranciscoA 1:57.86

Mixed Over 160 pounds
Gold: San Francisco A 2:35.13

400 Freestyle Relay
Mixed Under 120 pounds
Gold: San Francisco A 3:41.04
Silver: S.F. Rec. & Park 3:49.47
Bronze: San Diego A 4:36.50

Mixed Over 120 pounds
Gold: W.Hollywood 3:51.45
Silver: Berkeley, Ca. 4:19.42
Bronze: San Francisco 4:44.82

DIVING

One Meter (in points)
20 to 29 427.80
30 to 39 448.75
40 to 49 151.35

BASKETBALL

WOMEN
Gold: San Francisco
Silver: Los Angeles
Bronze: Denver

MEN
Gold: San Diego
Silver: San Francisco
Bronze: Los Angeles

SOFTBALL

WOMEN
Gold: San Francisco
Silver: Guerneville, Ca.
Bronze: Redwood City, Ca.

MEN
Gold: San Francisco
Silver: Boston
Bronze: Seattle

SOCCER

WOMEN		MEN	
Gold:	San Francisco	Gold:	San Francisco
Silver:	Vancouver	Silver:	New York
Bronze:	Berkeley, Ca.	Bronze:	Phoenix

VOLLEYBALL

WOMEN		MEN--'B' Divsion	
Gold:	Vancouver	Gold:	Toronto
Silver:	Berkeley, Ca.	Silver:	San Diego
Bronze:	Seattle	Bronze:	Seattle

MEN--"A" Divsion	
Gold:	Miami
Silver:	Seattle
Bronze:	Los Angeles

BOWLING

WOMEN		MIXED DOUBLES	
Gold:	Nicasio, Ca.	Gold:	San Jose, Ca.
Silver:	San Jose, Ca.	Silver:	San Francisco
Bronze:	San Francisco	Bronze:	San Jose, Ca.

MEN	
Gold:	Atlanta, Ga.
Silver:	West Hollywood, Ca.
Bronze:	Chicago

POOL

WOMEN--8 Ball Team		MEN--9Ball Team	
Gold:	San Francisco	Gold:	Sacramento, Ca.
Silver:	Bellaire, Tex.	Silver:	Houston
Bronze:	Brisbane, Ca.	Bronze:	Boston

MEN--8 Ball Team	
Gold:	Houston
Silver:	Sacramento, Ca.
Bronze:	Cloverdale, Ca.

INDIVIDUAL COMPETITION

Women:
- 8 Ball
- 9 Ball

Men:
- 8 Ball
- 9 Ball

MARATHON

WOMEN		MEN	
18 to 29	3:09:15	18 to 29	2:35:24
30 to 34	3:16:50	30 to 34	2:51:42
35 to 39	3:37:47	35 to 39	2:49:21
40 to 44	3:39:55	40 to 44	2:51:59
45 to 49	4:21:19	45 to 49	3:14:23
50 to 59	4:06.14	50 to 59	3:17:14

GOLF

WOMEN--Low Net		MEN--Low Net	
Gold:	138	Gold:	122
Silver:	145	Silver:	130
Bronze:	146	Bronze:	141

WOMEN--Low Gross		MEN--Low Gross	
Gold:	185	Gold:	151
Silver:	188	Silver:	155
Bronze:	191	Bronze:	156

ADDITIONAL INDIVIDUAL COMPETITIONS & CATEGORIES

CYCLING--25 Mile Road Race

PHYSIQUE

Team

Gold:	Hayward, Ca.
Silver:	Sacramento
Bronze:	San Francisco

RACQUETBALL

TENNIS

WRESTLING

POWERLIFTING

Women:
- 52 Kilos
- 56 Kilos
- 60 Kilos
- 67.5 Kilos
- 75 Kilos
- 82.5 Kilos
- 90 Kilos

Men:
- 67.5 Kilos
- 75 Kilos
- 82.5 Kilos
- 90 Kilos
- 100 Kilos
- 110 Kilos

Photo: Graphics/Darlene

Preview of Gay Games III

Celebration '90: Gay Games III & Cultural Festival

Sponsored by

Metropolitan Vancouver Athletic & Arts Association

August 4 to 11, 1990

Vancouver, B.C., CANADA

Athletic Events:

Badminton
Basketball
Bowling
Billiards
Croquet
Cycling
Darts
Diving
Equestrian
Golf
Ice Hockey
Marathon
Martial Arts
Physique
Powerlifting
Racquetball
Soccer
Softball
(Fast and Slow)
Squash
Swimming
Tennis
Touch Football
Track & Field
Triathlon
Volleyball
Water Polo
Wrestling

Cultural Events

Opening & Closing
Ceremonies
Fantasy Ball
Film Festival
Dance Across America
Night of 1,000 Voices
Literary Festival
Women's Cultural Event
Theatre Festival
Band Concerts

(Proposed)

Video Festival • Visual Arts Exhibition • Folk Festival • Chamber Music Concerts • Square Dance & Clogging • Opera • Crafts Bazaar • Chefs of the World

Ceremonies will be in B.C. Stadium

Registration

July 1, 1989, to Jan. 31, 1990. Fee: $36.00 U.S. ($40.00 Canadian)

Feb. 1, 1990 to May 31, 1990. Fee: $54.00 U.S. ($60.00 Canadian)
No registrations will be accepted after May 31, 1990

Forms are available at local gay/lesbian athletic associations or write:

Metropolitan Vancouver Athletic & Arts Assn.
1170 Bute St.
Vancouver, B.C., CANADA, V6E 1Z6
604-684-3303

EVENT OF THE YEAR:

Stonewall 20: A Generation of Pride Celebration in New York City June 1989

On Sunday, June 25, 1989, 150,000 marchers in New York City's Gay and Lesbian Pride Parade stepped off--with bands and banners, balloons and floats--and headed off down the length of Fifth Ave. to Greenwich Village and the Stonewall Inn, site of the historic riots in 1969 that sparked the modern gay/lesbian rights movement. The participants came from all over the country--bands from Denver and Washington, D.C., spectators from San Francisco, Chicago, and Atlanta.

Fifth Ave. has seen many parades commemorating many historic events: It was the route taken by American armies returning triumphant from World Wars I and II; by Charles Lindbergh after flying across the Atlantic Ocean; by astronauts after landing on the moon. And on that June day it was the route marched by gay and lesbian people celebrating a significant milestone in their history and their struggle for human rights--the passing of 20 years since gays and lesbians stood up to harassment by the police and symbolically said, "We won't take this anymore."

And hence the name of the 1989 celebration staged by New York's Heritage of Pride, "Stonewall 20: A Generation of Pride."

The weekend celebration included dances, parties, and concerts, a candlelight AIDS vigil, and a huge Celebration 20! rally Saturday afternoon in Central Park. A special stamp cancellation on Sunday commemorated the 20th annual gay pride day; a mobile U.S. Postal Service Unit set up shop in Sheridan Square, a park across from the site of the Stonewall Inn. The historic stamps depicted Walt Whitman or Eleanor Roosevelt. The cancellation read "Stonewall Station, 20 Years 1969-1989, Lesbian & Gay Pride, June 25, 1989, New York NY 10199."

There were also some unofficially scheduled events. A Saturday night reenactment of the police raid on the Stonewall Inn, with some participants dressed as cops and others carrying styrofoam bricks, almost deteriorated into a real riot as more than 1,000 people joined in, blocking streets in Greenwich Village. Earlier that day, thousands of gays and lesbians marched up Sixth Ave. to the rally in Central Park. But the demonstrations ended peacefully, and the weekend celebration concluded with a dance for thousands at the Christopher St. pier highlighted by a fireworks display over the river.

With balloons and bands, New York City's 1989 Gay/Lesbian Pride Parade, celebrating the 20th anniversary of the Stonewall riots, steps off from Columbus Circle and heads for Fifth Ave.

Photos by Envoy

"Stonewall 20: A Generation of Pride" was celebrated not only in New York, but all across America. In Chicago, a new generation of mayor, Richard M. Daley, joined some 90,000 gays and lesbians in that city's parade--a gesture that would have been unthinkable for his father, who was mayor 20 years before, and under whose administration police regularly raided gay bars.

Record Attendance at Gay/Lesbian Pride Celebrations

Stonewall 20 celebrations drew record crowds in such gay meccas as Los Angeles and San Francisco. But just as significantly, several cities in 1989 held their first public gay/lesbian pride celebrations. A crowd estimated at between 15,000 and 30,000 marched to the state capitol in Austin, Tex., on April 30 demanding laws guaranteeing gay/lesbian rights. Some 7,000 gays and lesbians on May 6 staged the first Pride Parade in Madison, Wisc. On June 17, an estimated 2,000 gays and lesbians marched in Milwaukee, Wisc., a city that had not had a Pride Parade in many years. And in Cleveland, Ohio, gays and lesbians on June 18 put on a Pride '89 street celebration in front of their new Lesbian/Gay Community Service Center.

Stonewall 20: A Generation of Pride was truly a nationwide--even a worldwide--event. But it was in New York City that it all began, and it is in New York City's Greenwich Village that the monument to this revolution stands. Twenty years later, all that remained of the Stonewall Inn was a black and white sign hanging on a building that by 1989 had become home to a Chinese restaurant. Across the street, Sheridan Square, where the gays gathered to hoot and throw bottles at the police raiders, is a peaceful triangle of green trees and red brick walkways. The block of Christopher St. on which the Stonewall building stands was renamed Stonewall Place during a Pride Week ceremony by the mayor of New York.

A Major Newspaper Series in San Francisco

Meanwhile, on the other side of the continent another significant event took place, this one in the press. The straight press has not been noted for thorough coverage of gay/lesbian issues. After the 1969 Stonewall Riots, there was only the briefest mention in the New York papers, and there are no records of the original Stonewall incident to be found in the news indexes or other standard research resources. But in 1989, a generation later, the *San Francisco Examiner* ran a 16-part series on being gay in America. They conducted an extensive survey, polling 3,748 self-identified straights and 400 self-identified gays or bisexuals nationwide between March 27 and April 17. The nationwide poll's margin of error was plus or minus 1.7 percentage points. They conducted a similar survey in the San Francisco Bay area of 1,871 straights and 400 gays or bisexuals.

As reflected in the surveys conducted for the *Examiner* series, a great many things have changed in America during one generation of pride--and then again, some things haven't. Finding people willing to say they were gay was still a problem. The *Examiner* ran this commentary with the series: "In an ap-

A Generation of Gays and Lesbians Has Largely Come Out of the Closet

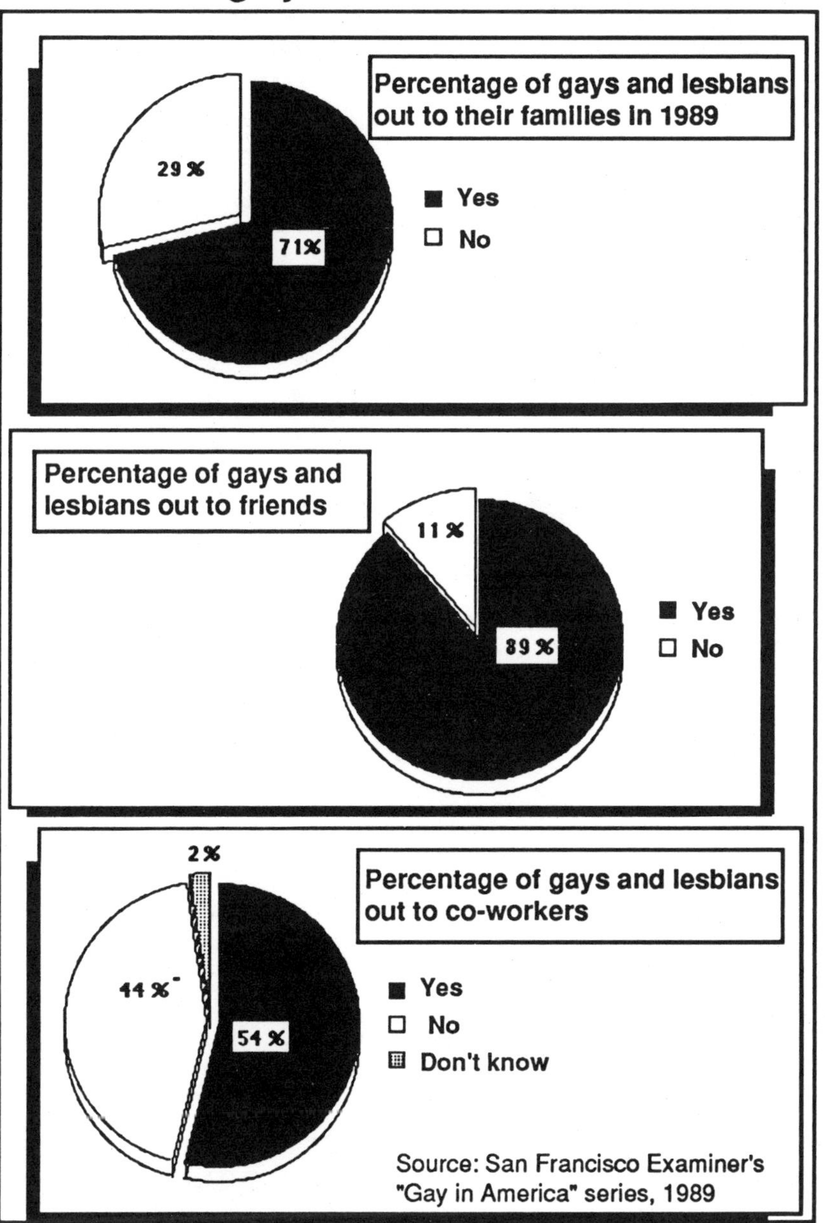

Stable, Long-Term Relationships Formed by Most Gay Men and Lesbians

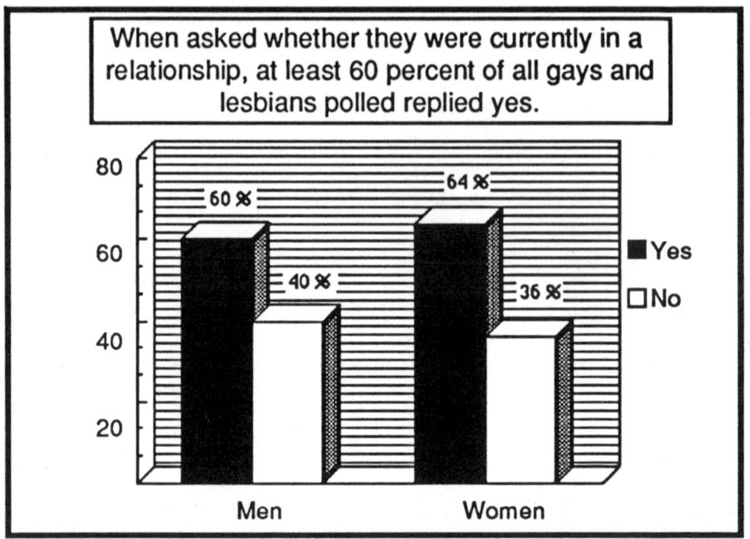

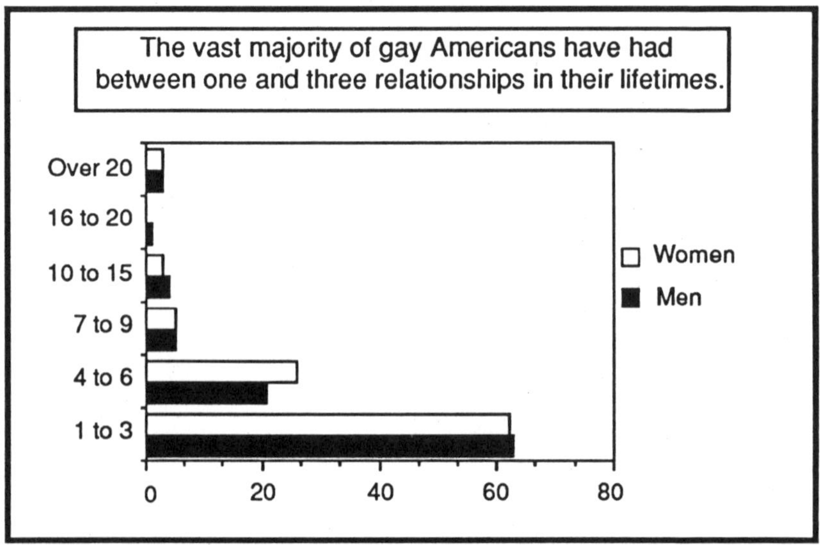

Source: San Francisco Examiner's "Gay in America" series, 1989

parent indication of continuing stigma attached to homosexuality, (the) random national poll found only 6.2 percent of those surveyed willing to tell a stranger over the phone that he or she was gay or bisexual.

"Only in the Bay Area did the number of people willing to say they were gay reach 10 percent (the commonly accepted percentage of people presumed to be gay). In small Midwestern states and in the South,... the rate was much lower than the national average....In Kansas, it took poll researchers nine full days of random dialing to find a single person who would say he was gay."

The Second Generation of Gays & Lesbians See a Better Life

Nevertheless, the survey found that two out of three gay Americans believe that life is getting better in terms of discrimination. About 70 percent are out to their families, and some 90 percent are out to straight friends. But, on the job they are less comfortable; less than half are open about their sexuality with co-workers.

The *Examiner* survey also found that the reality of gay and lesbian relationships belies the myth of emotional and affectional instability. Half of the gay Americans polled in 1989 had been in a stable relationship for at least two years. Gays are also stable economically. Only 2 percent were unemployed, and the average gay/lesbian income was above the national average. The average gay income was $29,129 annually and the average lesbian income $26,331, while the national average for a male head of household is $24,556; for a female head of household, $13,660.

In terms of straight attitudes toward gays and lesbians, the *Examiner* survey found some striking differences between theory and practice. A whopping 81 percent of the straights polled said that denying a person a job because of sexual orientation would be discriminatory. And most people agree that homosexuality should be legal; only 18 percent said it should be illegal. However, only 38 percent of these straights approved of a gay or lesbian couple living together in a marriagelike relationship, and 57 percent disapproved.

Regional differences were quite pronounced. The West was the most tolerant of gays and lesbians. In the San Francisco Bay Area, 52 percent of the straights polled approved of same-sex couples living together. The South, however, was the least tolerant with two-thirds of the straights disapproving of such living arrangements.

And so, it seems safe to conclude that despite enormous progress over an entire generation, gays and lesbians still have a long way to go in winning legal rights, family rights, and overall societal acceptance. **Danni Munson**

Reprints of the Examiner's "Gay in America" series are available (including a poster) for $5.00. Send your name, address, and phone number along with a check or money order to Gay in America Reprint, 943 Howard St. #304, San Francisco CA 94103. They will also accept VISA and MasterCard if you include your card number, expiration date, and your signature.

Arts and Entertainment
and the gay/lesbian world

A number of incidents during the year signalled that homophobia was alive and doing exceptionally well in the art and entertainment world. Conservative senators tried to ban funding for art judged to be obscene; right-wing elements fought to prevent positive images of gays and lesbians on television; and hate-inspiring remarks were made by several performers. Nevertheless, gay films and plays debuted, gay theaters thrived, and gay cable television continued to make inroads in major markets.

Mapplethorpe Exhibit Cancelled

A photography exhibit called "Robert Mapplethorpe: The Perfect Moment" arrived in Washington, D.C., in June 1989. Having already toured Philadelphia and Chicago, the exhibit, which included a number of explicitly gay, erotic photographs, was scheduled to open at the Corcoran Gallery of Art. But Senators Jesse Helms (R-N.C.) and Alphonse D'Amato (R-N.Y.), among others, cracked their moral whips and cried out in Congress that the exhibit was obscene. Faced with conservative pressure, the Corcoran closed its doors to Mapplethorpe (who had died of AIDS in March) and refused to allow the exhibit to go on. Several artists later refused to have their work shown there, and the curator of the Mapplethorpe exhibit resigned. In September 1989, the Corcoran announced it would publicly apologize for the cancellation.

Meanwhile, Helms spearheaded a drive in the Senate to bar funding of "obscene or indecent" artwork, including depictions of homoerotic artwork. The Senate passed the Helms measure on July 26. Many artists and supporters of the arts were outraged at this government meddling. The House rejected the Helms amendment, but a joint commmittee on September 29 agreed to a one-year ban on federal funds for "obscene" art.

Homophobia and the Media

Neanderthal humor on a recording by Sam Kinison and AIDS-phobia on the TV show "Midnight Caller" brought to birth in early 1989 the "Campaign for Fairness in Entertainment," founded by the National Gay and Lesbian Task Force, the Gay and Lesbian Alliance Against Defamation, and the New York Chapter of the National Organization for Women.

Kinison's Warner Brothers album, "Have You Seen Me Lately?", manages to insult gay men, lesbians, blacks, straight women, and especially people with AIDS. The "Midnight Caller" episode depicted a bisexual man with AIDS intentionally infecting both men and women with the AIDS-causing virus. Another album available during the year, this one from CBS

Records, called "Homesick Heros" by the Charlie Daniels Band, has a song entitled "Uneasy Rider '88," with lyrics that might be attractive to Nazis and other thugs. Another offender was Guns N Roses heavy metal band.

Right-wing religious groups were busy during the year trying to make sure that positive portrayals of lesbians and gay men were kept off the air waves. The ABC series "Heartbeat," which featured a healthy lesbian character, was the target of a hate-mail campaign conducted by the fundamentalist American Family Association. The AFA decided that a program with a well-adjusted lesbian involved in a positive same-sex relationship was "objectionable to traditional family values." The show was cancelled in the 1989 fall line-up because of low viewership, according to ABC.

A TV commercial for Kellogg's Nut 'N Honey cereal drew criticism during the year for being homophobic. In it rough-and-tumble cowboys drew their guns on the trail cook when he told them there was "nuttin honey" for breakfast. At Kellogg's annual stockholders' meeting in April 1989, 70-year-old Joseph Norton, claiming to be a relative of the founding Kellogg family, stood up and told the business gathering: "Some of us gay males have been rather upset by this commercial. We believe the company should be opposed to pulling a gun on anyone's head for any reason."

Comedian Bob Hope made a public service announcement against anti-gay violence that began airing on local TV stations in mid-1989. Hope made the public service announcement at the behest of the Gay and Lesbi-

"I Wish I Could Give it to Them" Awards

by Waldemar Bojczuk

Awards are everywhere in the entertainment world, Oscars, Emmys, Tonys. But there are a few categories I would like to see added this year to cover some very special areas.

"Joseph Goebbel's Award for Censorship in the Arts"--to Jesse Helms for protecting America against indecent artwork.

"Let's Grovel and Snivel Before the Congressional Inquisition" Award--to the Corcoran Gallery of Art for refusing to show the Robert Mapplethorpe exhibit.

"I Gotta Beat Up Fags to Prove I'm a Man" Award--to Charlie Daniels Band for the homophobic song "Uneasy Rider '88."

"Congratulatory Citation from the Spanish Inquisition" to the right-wing fundamentalist American Family Association for raging that a positive image of a healthy lesbian on television was objectionable to traditional family values.

an Alliance Against Defamation in New York City. GLAAD contacted Hope after hearing him make an inflammatory comment about gays on "The Tonight Show."

Gay/Lesbian Shows and Stations

Several gay/lesbian TV shows or shows with gay themes, in addition to those already mentioned, were broadcast during the year. In February, England saw the debut of its first gay TV show, "Out on Tuesday." In March, NBC aired "The Women of Brewster Place." The two-part miniseries, starring Oprah Winfrey, dealt with the not-unrelated themes of lesbianism and anti-gay prejudice and violence.

The student-run TV station at Stanford University in California in May presented a game show similar to the "Dating Game"--but with an important difference. All the contestants were gay.

The New York based Gay Cable Network expanded its area during the year. In April, Chicago became the eighth city to carry GCN programs. The other cities are Atlanta, Cincinnati, Los Angeles, Nashville, New Orleans, and San Francisco.

Gay/Lesbian Performing Arts

While the dance troupe "Les Ballets Trockadero de Monte Carlo" was flouncing once again from state to state and the gay musical "La Cage aux Folles" was still doing a high kick at many local dinner theaters, Harvey Fierstein's "Torch Song Trilogy" became the gay film of the year. Fierstein originally wrote "Torch Song" as a play. It had a successful run on Broadway and won a Tony Award in 1984. "Torch Song," the movie, was released in December 1988 and stars Fierstein, the actor, playing Arnold the drag queen, with Anne Bancroft playing his mother.

Across the length and breadth of the United States, theater and concert benefits were held to raise money for combatting AIDS. Plays dealing with AIDS also continued to proliferate.

New gay/lesbian theaters and theater groups appeared on both coasts. Theater BOBO opened in Washington, D.C., in early in 1989. In San Diego, a new women's group, Beautiful Lesbian Thesbians, began performing in October 1989.

Meanwhile, Olivia Records celebrated its 15th anniversary in November 1988 with a concert of women's music at New York City's Carnegie Hall. The 2,800-seat auditorium was sold out for the concert, headlined by Chris Williamson, and afterward some 1,500 women--all "dyked" out in evening gowns and tuxedos--gave the Grand Ballroom of the Waldorf-Astoria Hotel a night truly to remember.

Waldemar Bojczuk

GALA Choruses

The Gay and Lesbian Association of Choruses

GALA Choruses serves as an "information clearing house" for 72 gay/lesbian choruses in the United States and Canada. GALA Choruses sponsors annual conferences for directors and managers and produces a choral festival every three years. A festival was held in Seattle in July 1989. The next choral festival will take place in Denver in July 1992.

Below is a lising of member choruses as of July 1989

Artemis Singers
PO Box 578296
Chicago IL 60657

Atlanta Feminist Women's Chorus
Atlanta GA

Atlanta Gay Men's Chorus
PO Box 77114
Atlanta GA 30357
404-378-9676

Atlanta Lambda Choral
PO Box 7405
Atlanta GA 30357
404-874-1622

Anna Crusis Women's Choir
Philadelphia PA

Alamo Men's Chorale
San Antonio TX

Baltimore Gay Men's Chorus
PO Box 2401
Baltimore MD 21203-2401
301-828-0060

Boston Gay Men's Chorus
Box 1348 Back Bay Annex
Boston MA 02117
617-482-2527

Calliope Women's Chorus
3353 31st Ave. S.
Minneapolis MN 55406
612-377-1611

Champaign-Urbana Men's Chorus
2304 C Melrose Dr.
Champaign IL 61820

Chicago Gay Men's Chorus
PO Box 14146
Chicago IL 60614
312-477-9380

City of Good Neighbors Chorale
Ellicott Sta. PO Box 556
Buffalo NY 14205-0556
716-886-0102

Connecticut Gay Men's Chorus
480 Winthrop Ave.
New Haven CT 06511
203-787-2835

Cream City Chorus
124 N. Water St.
Milwaukee WI 53202
414-227-0434

Dayton Men's Chorus
1362 Harvard Blvd
Dayton OH 45406
513-274-4749

Denver Gay Men's Chorus
PO Box 671
Denver CO 80206
303-331-2302

Denver Women's Chorus
PO Box 2638
Denver CO 80202
303-447-8702

Des Moines Men's Chorus
1534 47th St.
Des Moines IA 50311
515-255-1684

Detroit Together Men's Chorus
PO Box 1381
Berkeley MI 48072
313-280-3872

Fest City Singers
PO Box 11428
Milwaukee WI 53211-0428
414-476-7464

Gay Men's Chorus of Long Beach
2017 E 4th St.
Long Beach CA 90814
213-434-6093

Gay Men's Chorus of Los Angeles
7985 Santa Monica Blvd.
#109-134
W. Hollywood CA 90046
213-462-5284

Gay Men's Chorus of South Florida
12555 Biscayne Blvd. #822
Miami FL 33181-2597
305-757-7464

Gay Men's Chorus of Washington
PO Box 57043
Washington DC 20037
202-546-1549

Golden Gate Men's Chorus
116 Eureka St.
San Francisco CA 94114
415-626-2883

Heartland Men's Chorus
PO Box 32374
Kansas City MO 6411
816-561-5602

Honolulu Men's Chorus
c/o Gay Community Center
Box 3224
Honolulu HI 96801
808-536-6000

Kansas City Women's Chorus
Kansas City MO

Lansing Women's Chorus
412 Lathrop
Lansing MI 48912

Lesbian/Gay Chorus of S.F.
584 Castro St. #284
San Francisco CA 94114
415-586-8022

Los Angeles Women's Community Chorus
20423 Raymond Ave.
Torrence CA 90502
213-715-1281

Madison Gay Men's Chorale
Memorial Union PO Box 605
Madison WI 53706

Maiden Voyage
Milwaukee WI

Montrose Chamber Singers
1216 Peden #3
Houston TX 77006
713-526-3810

MUSE Cincinnati Women's Chorus
4260 Langland
Cincinnati OH 45223
513-541-0560

New Mexico Gay Men's Chorus
8640 Horatio Pl. NE
Albuquerque MN 87111
505-296-9215

New Orleans Gay Men's Chorus
PO Box 19365
New Orleans LA 70119-9365
504-324-2987

New York City Gay Men's Chorus
PO Box 587
New York NY 10156
212-691-7590

One Voice Mixed Chorus
Minneapolis MN

Ottawa Men's Chorus
1865 Longman Crescent
Orleans, Ontario
Canada K1C 5H4

Philadelphia Gay Men's Chorus
PO Box 58842
Philadelphia PA 19102
215-732-5079

Portland Gay Men's Chorus
PO Box 3223
Portland OR 97208
503-227-7907

Portland Lesbian Choir
PO Box 8212
Portland OR 97208
503-231-9351

PRIDE
San Fernando CA

Queen City Men's Chorale
4300 Leeper
Cincinnati OH 45223-1924
513-541-0003

Renaissance City Choir
PO Box 10282
Pittsburgh PA 15232
412-242-5539

Rhode Island Men's Chorus
25 Parade St. #3
Providence RI 02909

River City Mixed Chorus
PO Box 315
Omaha NE 68101
402-341-0763

Rochester Gay Men's Chorus
PO Box 1892
Rochester NY 14603
716-235-2473

Sacramento Men's Chorus
920 Snyder Dr.
Davis CA 95616
916-756-8120

Saint Louis Women's Choir
St. Louis MO

Salt Lake City Men's Choir
Salt Lake City UT

Santa Cruz Men's Chorus
Santa Cruz CA
408-427-2722

San Diego Men's Chorus
PO Box 33825
San Diego CA 92103
619-296-4054

San Diego Women's Chorus
6951 Princess View Dr.
San Diego CA 92103
619-265-2877

San Francisco Gay Men's Chorus
PO Box 421491
San Francisco CA 94142
415-864-0326

Seattle Women's Ensemble
Seattle WA

Seattle Men's Chorus
PO Box 2521
Seattle WA 98111

Silicon Valley Gay Men's Chorus
361 Greenpark Way
San Jose CA 95136
408-374-3767

Spruce St. Singers
28 Woodhurst Dr.
West Berlin NJ 08091
609-435-0826

Stonewall Chorale (Mixed)
PO Box 920
New York NY 10011-0901
212-721-2924

Tacoma Women's Choir
PO Box 7426
Tacoma WA 98407
206-759-3795

Tampa Bay Gay Men's Chorus
Tampa Bay FL

Toronto Men's Chorus
2 Bloor St. W. #100
Toronto, Ontario
Canada M4W 3E2
416-461-0517

Tucson Metropolitan Community Chorus
Tucson AZ

Turtle Creek Chorale
PO Box 190806
Dallas TX 75219-0806
214-526-3214

Twin Cities Men's Chorus
528 Hennepin Ave. #208
Minneapolis MN 55403
612-336-4079

Vancouver Men's Chorus
1270 Chestnut St.
Vancouver, B.C.
Canada V6J 4R9
604-669-7464

West Coast Singers
7236 Fountain Ave. #16
West Hollywood
CA 90046-5732
213-874-2837

Windy City Gay Chorus
606 W. Barry #216
Chicago IL 60657
312-404-9242

Womyn's Chorus of South Florida

Books

of Interest to Gay Men and Lesbians

Visibility: high; outlook: good. Gay and lesbian literature bursts into the 90's on solid ground. Though 1988 proved to be a turning point in the direction and quality of gay and lesbian writing, 1989 set our literature in front of the public eye and allowed us to pat ourselves on the back. While only the coming days will show how successful we've been at improving our collective craft and attracting a far-reaching and diverse readership, the books and events of the past year certainly pay tribute to a flourishing and unique area of literature.

The most significant affirmations came in the form of awards for excellence in gay and lesbian literature. The Lambda Literary Awards program, instituted by *Lambda Rising BOOK REPORT* in 1989 to reward and promote the progress being made by gay and lesbian writers and publishers, premiered at the American Booksellers Association Convention in Washington, DC, on June 2nd. Emceed by author Armistead Maupin, the awards banquet was attended by more than 300 writers, publishers, booksellers, editors, media reps, and readers, as well as national gay and lesbian figures. Author Edmund White receivd a lifetime achievement award.

Recipients of the First Annual
LAMBDA LITERARY AWARDS

Gay Men's Nonfiction: **Borrowed Time,** Paul Monette
Lesbian Fiction: **Trash,** Dorothy Allison
Lesbian Small Press Book Award: **Trash,** Dorothy Allison
Gay Men's Fiction: **The Beautiful Room is Empty,** Edmund White
Gay Men's Mystery/Science Fiction: **Goldenboy,** Michael Nava
Gay Men's Small Press Book Award: (tie) **Goldenboy,** Michael Nava and **The Delight of Hearts,** Ahmad El-Tifashi
Lesbian Nonfiction: **Lesbian Ethics,** Sarah Hoagland
Lesbian Mystery/Science Fiction: **Skiptrace,** Antoinette Azolakov
Gay Men's First Novel: **The Swimming-Pool Library,** Alan Hollinghurst
Lesbian First Novel: **Bird-Eyes,** Madelyn Arnold
Gay and Lesbian Poetry: **Gay & Lesbian Poetry in Our Time,** Carl Morse and Joan Larkin, eds.
AIDS (a special category): **Borrowed Time,** Paul Monette
Publisher's Service Award: Sasha Alyson of Alyson Publications for his work on the industry-wide book project, **You Can Do Something About AIDS**
Editor's Choice Award: **Why Can't Sharon Kowalski Come Home?,** Karen Thompson and Julie Andrzejewski

Other accolades came from very different organizations. At a strained ceremony held in New York in May, the very mainstream Academy of American Poets presented the prestigious Lamont Prize to lesbian poet Minnie Bruce Pratt for a forthcoming collection entitled **A Crime Against Nature.** On a different coast in March, the inter-community Words Project for AIDS recognized excellence in AIDS-related writing, conferring honors on gay and mainstream titles alike, including **AIDS: the Women** edited by Ines Rieder and Patricia Ruppelt (Nonfiction) and Paul Monette's **Love Alone: 18 Elegies for Rog** (Poetry/Fiction). The Publishing Triangle, a caucus of gays and lesbians in the publishing trade formed in 1989, presented the First Annual Bill Whitehead Award for lifetime achievement in gay writing to Edmund White. Winning the American Library Association honors this year for best gay books were Sarah Schulman's **After Delores** and Alan Hollinghurst's first novel, **The Swimming-Pool Library.**

The erotica trend in lesbian literature, which reached a new peak in late 1988 with **Macho Sluts,** continued in 1989 with the publication of Tee Corinne's **Lovers,** the Sheba Collective's **Serious Pleasure,** Terry Woodrow's **Lesbian Bedtime Stories,** and editor Susie Bright's **Herotica,** among others.

The big men's books of 1989 included Armistead Maupin's final installment in the *Tales of the City* series, **Sure of You**; David Leavitt's well-crafted but tame look into gay yuppie-dom, **Equal Affections**; editor George Stambolian's second compilation of fine short fiction by talented and, for the most part, established male writers, **Men on Men 2**; Alyson Publication's ethnically diverse and more daring small press counterpart to *Men on Men 2*, **Shadows of Love**, edited by Charles Jurrist; Christopher Bram's poignant AIDS novel, **In Memory of Angel Clare**; and C.F. Borgman's stunning debut, **River Road.**

Other bestselling novels included Ethan Mordden's tale of gay Manhattan and Fire Island, **Everybody Loves You**; Dennis Cooper's haunting **Closer**; Kevin Killian's notable first try, **Shy**; M.S. Hunter's pirate story, **The Buccaneer**; Steve Kluger's baseball yarn, **Changing Pitches**; and a first novel about one black young man's struggle to live with his gayness, Randall Keenan's **A Visitation of Spirits.**

As usual, lesbians excelled in the nonfiction department. Sarah Lucia Hoagland supplied the year's finest work with **Lesbian Ethics: Toward New Value** and **For Lesbians Only: A Separatist Anthology** (co-edited by Julia Penelope). In late 1988, Karen Thompson and Julie Andrzejewski chronicled Karen's struggle to see and take care of her disabled life partner Sharon in **Why Can't Sharon Kowalski Come Home?** Christine Downing retrieved a deeper understanding of gay love in **Myths and Mysteries of Same-Sex Love.** Martha Barron Barrett's travelogue of the Lesbian Nation, **Invisible Lives**, sought to educate the mainstream about the invisibility of women-loving women. Sonia Johnson planned for the "she/volution" in **Wildfire**, while Judy Grahn critiqued the work of a historical lesbian figure in **Really Reading Gertrude Stein.**

Observers of lesbian literature can gauge its progress by keeping an eye on the world's most successful lesbian publisher, Naiad Press. And, indeed, Naiad had a banner year with the publication of 24 books. Jane Rule followed up last year's critically acclaimed **Memory Board** with this year's insightful story of loss and new beginnings, **After the Fire**. Katherine Forrest fans were treated to the third (and best) Kate Delafield mystery, **The Beverly Malibu**. Naiad Press responded by making **Malibu** its first exclusive hardback title.

Count in the notable works of fiction Nisa Donnelly's **The Bar Stories**, about a legendary lesbian bar and its patrons; May Sarton's story of a 60-year-old lesbian opening a women's bookstore, **The Education of Harriet Hatfield**; Jan Clausen's well-crafted **The Prosperine Papers**; Shay Youngblood's first collection, **The Big Mama Stories**; Valerie Miner's short stories, **Trespassing**; and Adrienne Rich's latest collection of poetry, **Time's Power**. Rita Mae Brown, on the other hand, provided a bit of irony late last year: she celebrated the 15th anniversary of **Rubyfruit Jungle** by writing **Bingo**, a disappointing novel in which the lesbian protagonist sleeps with her best friend's husband and bears his child.

Hands down, the most controversial title of 1989 was **After the Ball: How America Will Conquer Its Fear & Hatred of Gays in the 90s**. In this weighty book (published and widely promoted, incidentally, by mainstream publisher Doubleday), gay social scientists Hunter Madsen and Marshall Kirk assert that the gay liberation movement was a bust, and that drag queens and butches will have to go back in the closet before straights will accept gays and lesbians in the coming decade. The national advertising campaign that the two men devised for use by gay and lesbian organizations is commendable, but the general dismissal of gay activist work of the past two decades is insulting at best.

AIDS continued to play a big part in the gay literature scene. Angry AIDS activist Larry Kramer addressed the realities of AIDS in **Reports from the Holocaust**, while Susan Sontag took a more philosophical look at the epidemic in **AIDS and Its Metaphors.** In **Poets for Life**, editor Michael Klein collected poets' responses to AIDS, while John Preston presented those of writers in **Personal Dispatches: Writers Confront AIDS.** Tim Barrus gave us little hope in his collection of writings about AIDS, **Genocide**. Important fiction responses included Christopher Davis' first collection of short stories, **The Boys in the Bars**, Larry Duplechan's **Tangled Up in Blue**, David Feinberg's well-received AIDS "comedy," **Eighty-Sixed**, and Paul Reed's San Francisco chronicle, **Longing**. Two visual arts

GAY/LESBIAN BEST SELLERS

as of September 1989

MEN'S HARDBACKS

1. **AFTER THE BALL**, Marshall Kirk & Hunter Madsen, Doubleday, $19.95
2. **BEING HOMOSEXUAL,** Richard A. Isay, M.D., Farrar Straus Giroux, $14.95
3. **PERMANENT PARTNERS,** Betty Berzon, Ph.D., E.P. Dutton, $18.95
4. **SHORE LEAVE**, Andrew Kennedy, Bruno Gmünder, $25.95
5. **BUDDY'S: MEDITATIONS ON DESIRE,** Stan Persky, New Star Books, $16.95
6. **EIGHTY-SIXED,** David B. Feinberg, Viking, $18.95
7. **HOME BOY**, Jimmy Cheshire, New American Library, $18.95
8. **IN MEMORY OF ANGEL CLARE,** Christopher Bram, Donald I. Fine, $18.95

MEN'S PAPERBACKS

1. **ABOUT COURAGE**, Mickey C. Fleming, Holloway House, $2.95
2. **ON BEING GAY**, Brian McNaught, St. Martin's Press, $7.95
3. **BEAUTIFUL ROOM IS EMPTY**, Edmund White, Ballantine, $4.95
4. **MATLOVICH: THE GOOD SOLDIER**, Mike Hippler, Alyson Publications, $8.95
5. **HOLD TIGHT**, Christopher Bram, New American Library, $8.95
6. **GROUND ZERO**, Andrew Holleran, NAL, $7.95
7. **MEATMEN VOL. 5**, ed. Winston Leyland, Gay Sunshine Press, $12.95
8. **PANTHERS IN THE SKINS OF MEN**, Charles Nelson, Lyle Stuart, $9.95
9. **CHANGING PITCHES**, Steve Kluger, Alyson Publ., $7.95
10. **THE BUCCANEER**, M. S. Hunter, Alyson Publ., $8.95

WOMEN'S HARDBACKS

1. **PERMANENT PARTNERS,** Betty Berzon, E.P Dutton, $18.95
2. **BAR STORIES,** Nisa Donnelly, St. Martin's Press, $17.95
3. **TEMPLE OF MY FAMILIAR**, Alice Walker, Harcourt Brace Jovanovich, $19.95
4. **EDUCATION OF HARRIET HATFIELD**, May Sarton, Norton, $18.95
5. **SKID: A VIOLET CHILDES MURDER MYSTERY**, Maud Farrell, Dutton, $16.95
6. **INVISIBLE LIVES**, Martha Barron Barrett, Morrow, $19.95
7. **BRAZILIAN BOMBSHELL**, Martha Gil-Montero, Donald I. Fine, $18.95
8. **SHE CAME IN A FLASH**, Mary Wings, New American Library, $17.95

WOMEN'S PAPERBACKS

1. **LESBIAN BEDTIME STORIES**, Terry Woodrow, Tough Dove Books, $9.95
2. **LESBIAN LOVE STORIES**, ed. by Irene Zahava, Crossing Press, $9.95
3. **ASSISTANCE OF VICE**, Rosylyn Dane, Banned Books, $8.95
4. **EDGEWISE**, Camarin Grae, Naiad Press, $9.95
5. **LOVERS**, Tee Corinne, Banned Books, $7.95
6. **UNBROKEN TIES**, Carol Becker, Alyson Publications, $7.95
7. **DOG COLLAR MURDERS**, Barbara Wilson, Seal Press, $8.95
8. **SERIOUS PLEASURES**, ed. Sheba Collective, Sheba Feminist Publishers, $9.95
9. **LESBIAN COUPLES**, D. Merilee Clunis, Seal Press, $10.95
10. **KEEP TO ME, STRANGER**, Sarah Aldridge, Naiad Press, $9.95

Best sellers were determined by Lambda Rising's nationwide phone and mail order sales and by sales in Lambda Rising's Washington, DC, and Baltimore, MD, stores.

books attempted to capture the meaning of AIDS in that medium: **AIDS: Images for Survival** by the Shoshin Society, and photographer Billy Howard's **Epitaphs for the Living.** Rounding out gay men's nonfiction bestsellers are **In Search of Gay America** by Neil Miller, **Being Homosexual** by Richard Isay, and Mickey Fleming's **About Courage**.

Mysteries topped the lesbian bestsellers lists. Small presses gave us many enjoyable whodunits, including the previously mentioned **Beverly Malibu**; Claire McNab's **Fatal Reunion**; Barbara Wilson's **The Dog Collar Murders**; Antoinette Azolakov's **The Contactees Die Young**, and **The Second Womansleuth Anthology** edited by Irene Zahava. Some came from large publishing houses, including Mary Wings' **She Came in a Flash** and Maud Farrell's **Skid**, as well as the paperback edition of **After Delores.**

If laughter is the best medicine, we should be feeling fine. Humor books abounded with a book-length edition of **Gay Comics**, N. Leigh Dunlap's second Morgan Calabrese collection, **Run That Sucker at Six!!!**, and a delightful and witty offering, **Found Goddesses** by Julie Penelope and Morgan Grey. Self help books advised those in **Gay Relationships** (Tina Tessina) and gays and lesbians in twelve step programs (**Accepting Ourselves** by Sheppard Kominars). The year's steadiest seller to men *and* women was Betty Berzon's **Permanent Partners: Building Gay & Lesbian Relationships That Last.**

Biographies of lesbians were scarce this year, with Diane Souhami's portrait of painter **Glück** practically summing up the selection. Men, on the other hand, enjoyed literary biographies of Beat figures William Burroughs, Paul Bowles, and Allen Ginsberg. The 1987 death of "shy, bald, myopic, gay albino" Andy Warhol inspired a number of books including, most notably, **The Andy Warhol Diaries**. The story of gay military man Leonard Matlovich was published by Alyson Publications in late 1988.

In 1989, the literary community lost many of its greatest members: lesbian poet Pat Parker, literary legend James Baldwin, and lesbian archivist Bunny MacCulloch to cancer; and photographer Robert Mapplethorpe, French author Emmanuel Dreuilhe, playwright James Kirkwood, editor Joe Beam, poet Chasen Gaver, author Geoff Mains, and writer George Whitmore to AIDS.

The coming decade is already assured a good start, for new books by Sarah Schulman, David Leavitt, Michael Nava, Dorothy Allison, Eric Marcuc, and Andrew Holleran were already in the works. Certainly the greatest challenge for gay/lesbian writers and publishers in the 1990s will be to maintain the rate of progress they achieved during the 1980s.

Jane Troxell
editor, *Lambda Rising Book Report*

HEALTH ISSUES
affecting gays and lesbians

Concerns about AIDS continued to dominate gay/lesbian health issues during 1989. As the number of cases passed the 100,000 mark, a breakthrough in drug treatment reported in August promised to delay onset of symptoms in people testing positive for HIV, the virus that causes AIDS. AIDS activists were a powerful force at the annual AIDS conference in Montreal in June. Poppers were banned by an omnibus health bill passed in late 1988, and a National Commission on AIDS was established.

AZT Reportedly Delays Onset of AIDS Symptoms

The drug AZT can slow the onset of AIDS in people who have tested positive but not yet developed symptoms, according to two studies reported in August 1989. AZT inhibits replication of HIV. Because there now is apparently an effective treatment, the Department of Health and Human Services urged all high-risk individuals to be tested.

However, AZT is priced very high--up to $8,000 per year--and public health experts in autumn 1989 estimated that 600,000 people might qualify for the drug at a cost of $5 billion to $10 billion. In September there were protests against the British manufacturer of AZT, Burroughs Wellcome, in New York, San Francisco, and London, accusing the drug company of shameless profiteering. ACT UP members chained themselves to the balcony of the New York Stock Exchange and used sound equipment at the opening bell to urge traders to sell Wellcome stock.

A new drug, DDI, which is chemically related to AZT, showed promise of increasing immune system function without producing the side effects sometimes caused by AZT. The NIH in July 1989 announced it would try the drug on 2,000 volunteers. Scientists and activists alike hoped DDI would be less costly than AZT.

Another approach that showed promise involved making a drug from the CD 4 receptors that the virus uses to enter white blood cells. By using genetic engineering techniques to make millions of identical CD 4 receptors and injecting them into the body, researchers hoped to "tie up" the virus before it could attach to the real receptor on the cells.

New Drug Rules

New FDA regulations adopted in 1988 made it easier for people with AIDS to gain access to experimental drugs, especially those imported from other countries. But this loosening of rules also led to controversy. High

AIDS HOTLINES

The following is a listing of national AIDS hotlines and states that have AIDS hotline numbers. The hotlines provide information about the disease, testing centers, and where to seek treatment. Most numbers are toll-free.

National AIDS Hotline:
Tape: 800/342-AIDS
Operator: 800/342-7514

AIDS Treatment Hotline:
800/822-7422

Alabama: 800/445-3741
Arizona: 800/334-1540
Arkansas: 800/445-7720
California (northern)
800/367-2437
Connecticut: 203/566-1157
Delaware: 302/995-8422
District of Columbia: 202/332-AIDS
Florida: 800-FLA-AIDS
Georgia: 800/551-2728
Hawaii: 808/922-1313
Illinois: 800/243-2438
Iowa: 800/532-3301
Kansas: 800/232-0040
Kentucky: 800/654-AIDS
Louisiana: 800/992-4379
Maine: 800/851-AIDS
Maryland: 800/638-6252
Massachusetts: 800/235-2331
Michigan (Detroit Area): 800/872-AIDS
Minnesota: 800/248-AIDS
Mississippi: 800/826-2961
Nebraska: 800-782-2437
New Jersey: 800/624-2377
New York: 800/462-1884
North Dakota: 800/592-1861
Ohio: 800/332-AIDS
Pennsylvania: 800/692-7254
Rhode Island: 402-277-6502
South Carolina: 800/322-AIDS
South Dakota: 800/472-2180
Tennessee: 800/342-AIDS
Utah: 800/843-9388; 801/466-9976
Vermont: 800/882-AIDS
Virginia: 800-533-4148
West Virginia: 800/642-8244
Wisconsin: 800/334-AIDS

Cities in the United States and U.S. Territories Reporting a Total of More Than 1,000 AIDS Cases between 1981 and mid-1989

1. New York City.....20,561
2. Los Angeles...........7,256
3. San Francisco.........6,639
4. Houston..................3,015
5. Newark, N.J...........2,993
6. Washington, DC ...2,939
7. Miami 2,557
8. Chicago 2,543
9. Philadelphia 2,175
10. Atlanta, Ga. 1,910
11. Boston 1,756
12. Dallas 1,750
13. San Juan, P.R. 1,620
14. San Diego 1,383
15. Ft. Lauderdale ...1, 320
16. Jersey City, N.J. 1,267
17. Oakland, Calif. ...1,210
18. Nassau-Suffolk, N.Y......1,091
19. Seattle 1,028

Source: Centers for Disease Control: HIV/AIDS Surveillance Report, August 1989

doses of Compound Q, a drug made from a Chinese cucumber plant in legal but unauthorized experiments resulted in serious reactions, including the deaths of three volunteers between June and October 1989.

Federal health officials in July 1989 endorsed a drug-availability plan called parallel-track distribution. The plan would make new drugs available to seriously ill people as soon as the early Phase I safety testing was completed. Implementation of speedier drug delivery, however, was a cause for concern. AIDS activists met with federal officials in August 1989 to express dissatisfaction over what they regarded as unnecessary delays in getting parallel track standards.

AIDS Conference in Montreal

The Fifth International Conference on AIDS, held in Montreal, Canada, in June 1989 attracted about 12,000 health care professionals, 5,000 more than were present at the 1988 conference in Stockholm. At the conference was a highly visible presence of AIDS activists, especially the direct action group, ACT UP. The AIDS activists took over the stage just before the conference was to begin and made several demands, including that AIDS be treated as a chronic, manageable condition.

Public health experts attending the conference reported that the rate of increase of new AIDS cases was slowing among gay men, but increasing among other groups, especially intravenous drug abusers. The use of crack, a potent form of cocaine, was singled out as a major emerging AIDS risk factor--although an indirect one. Researchers have found that crack users obtain money for the drug by selling sex, a trend that was growing in low-income areas.

One ominous finding reported at the conference suggested that gay men might be returning to high-risk sexual practices, particularly anal intercourse without the protection of a condom.

In August 1989, organizers of the 1990 AIDS conference to be held in San Francisco announced attendance would be limited to 12,000 and only hard-science issues, not psychosocial issues, would be addressed.

Sexual Behavior Survey Needed

The topic of sexual behavior surveys became surrounded during the year with controversy--both scientific and political. The need for a thorough and thoughtful survey of the sexual behavior of Americans was expressed by the nation's leading scientists and scientific organizations. No good set of data exists on which predictions, for example, about the spread of AIDS can be based. Most estimates of sexuality are based on 1948 studies by biologist Alfred Kinsey, and social scientists point out that the people he interviewed were not randomly selected. Two additional Kinsey Institute studies released during the year raised important issues and pointed toward the need for good data.

The Profile of AIDS

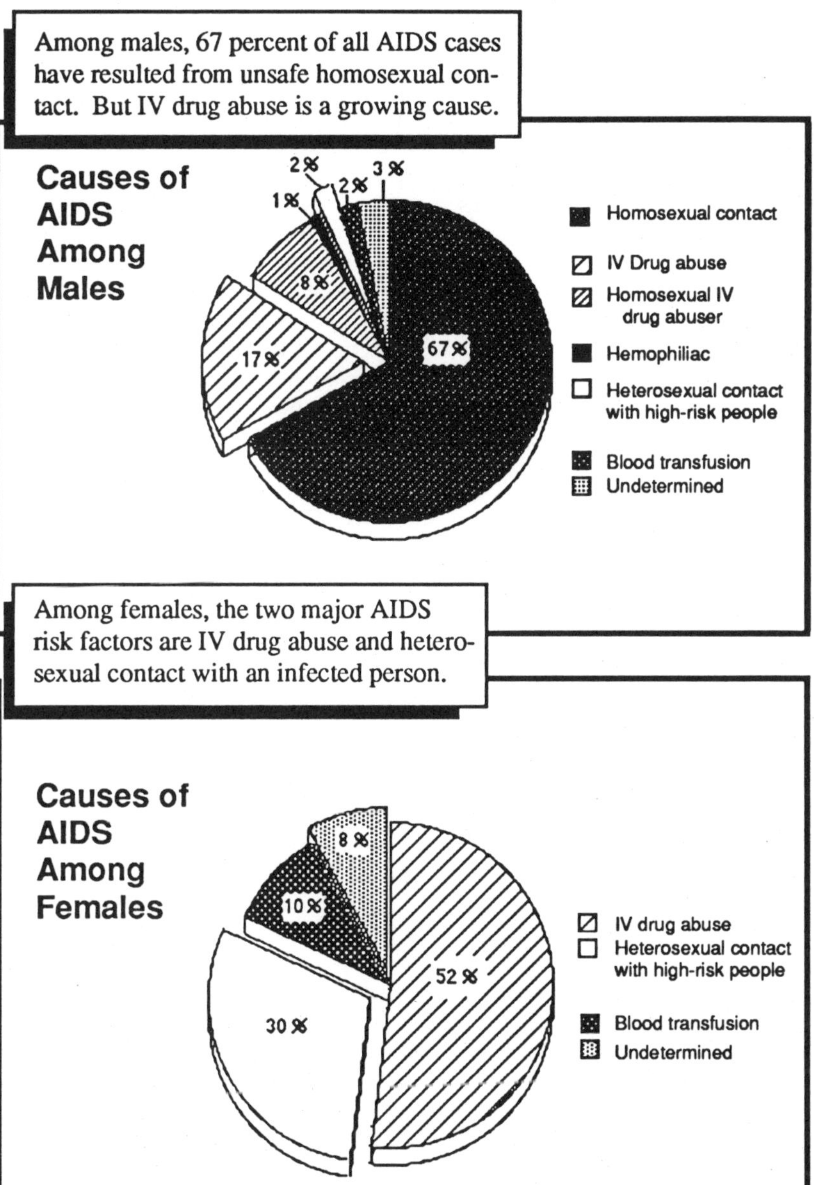

Source: Centers for Disease Control: HIV/AIDS Surveillance Report, August 1989

For example, self-identified sexuality is not by itself a good predictor of whether an individual has engaged in high-risk sexual activity, according to Kinsey Institute researcher June Reinisch. Of 262 self-identified lesbians interviewed at the Michigan Women's Music Festival in August 1987, about one-third said they had recently engaged in sex with bisexual men. A similar sampling of gay men revealed that up to 79 percent of them had had sex with a woman during the previous 12-month period.

Then, in the Jan. 20, 1989, issue of *Science* magazine, Kinsey Institute researchers published the results of a 1970 survey of 3,018 adults that seemed to show fewer adult males engage in homosexual activity than had been thought from estimates based on Kinsey's 1948 survey. The 1970 Kinsey Institute survey estimated that about 20 percent of males had at least one homosexual encounter and that 3.3 percent are exclusively gay. The 1948 data gave rise to estimates of 37 percent having at least one same-sex encounter and 4 percent being exclusively gay.

Publication of the 1970 survey was held up for almost 20 years because the scientists could not agree on how to interpret the data or on who should be credited as authors of the report. One major flaw in the 1970 data was that some 15 percent of the 1,450 men surveyed refused to answer questions on homosexuality. There were also questions in the 1970 survey about lesbianism, but this data was not reported.

Conservatives Block Sex Survey

Because of the lack of good data, the National Academy of Sciences (NAS) and its Institute of Medicine in 1987 had advised the federal government to conduct a broad, detailed survey of all human sexual behavior in the United States. The National Research Council of the NAS in February 1989 urged that the U.S. Public Health Service undertake such a survey to determine the extent of behavior that might put a person at risk for developing AIDS.

A unit of the National Institutes of Health did begin to develop a sexual behavior survey, and the Public Health Service planned a pilot test of questions and interview techniques to begin in March 1989. The survey, however, was sidetracked by right-wing elements in government.

Citing his responsibility to review the survey questions under the Federal Paperwork Reduction Act, Director of the Office of Management and Budget Richard Darman managed to hold up start of the pilot test for one month. Darmon objected to questions relating to oral and anal sexual practices, saying he doubted this would serve any "appropriate public purpose."

Then the matter was passed on to Health and Human Services Secretary Louis Sullivan, who on April 7 officially refused to allow the pilot program to begin. He said the Public Health Service could not conduct such a survey until there was a "thorough review and revision" of the questions.

The Toll of AIDS

AIDS Cases and AIDS Deaths
Among Adults and Adolescents
by Six-Month Reporting Periods Since 1981
Source: Centers for Disease Control
HIV/AIDS Surveillance Report, August 1989

Date of Diagnosis	Number of Cases	Number of Deaths
Before 1981	77	63
Jan. to June 1981	88	81
July to Dec. 1981	194	178
Jan. to June 1982	381	347
July to Dec. 1982	657	588
Jan. to June 1983	1,246	1,139
July to Dec. 1983	1,608	1,461
Jan. to June 1984	2,501	2,153
July to Dec. 1984	3,292	2,865
Jan. to June 1985	4,679	4,022
July to Dec. 1985	6,044	5,065
Jan. to June 1986	7,871	6,290
July to Dec. 1986	9,429	6,952
Jan. to June 1987	11,889	7,980
July to Dec. 1987	13,016	7,062
Jan. to June 1988	14,020	5,911
July to Dec. 1988	13,452	4,318
Jan. to July 1989	10,441	1,970
Total	**100,885**	**58,447**

States with the Greatest Number of Reported AIDS Cases *

1. New York
2. California
3. New Jersey
4. Florida
5. Texas

States with the Least Number of Reported AIDS Cases *

1.North Dakota
2. South Dakota
3. Montana
4. Alaska
5. Vermont

* August 1988 to July 1989

Right-wing politicians such as Congressman William Dannemeyer (R., Calif.) and Senator Jesse Helms (R., N.C.), applied pressure to do away with the survey entirely. Dannemeyer circulated a letter to members of Congress insinuating that the survey was intended solely to advance the gay/lesbian rights movement. "Imagine," said the letter, "the political landscape if any one demographic grouping were to increase their ranks from 10% of the population to 15% or 20%."

Apparently bowing to such conservative pressure, Sullivan said in June that he was referring the matter of the survey to an unnamed panel for review. Meanwhile, gay activists feared that Helms would introduce a measure in Congress prohibiting the use of federal funds for the survey.

Lesbian Health Survey

A columnist for Chicago OUTLINES in the May 1989 issue reported on a lesbian health survey listed in the second edition of *The Source Book on Lesbian and Gay Health Care*. The study analyzed the responses of 1,925 questionnaires filled out by self-identified lesbians in 1984-1985.

Among the finding about lesbian-related health issues were:

- Bad cramps was the main health problem of lesbians age 17 to 34.
- Breast lumps was the number-one concern of lesbians age 45 to 54.
- Only 10 percent were concerned they might be at risk for AIDS
- Almost 20 percent had attempted suicide
- 84 percent consumed alcohol; 47 percent smoked marijuana; 20 percent used cocaine
- 41 percent smoked tobacco
- 21 percent had been sexually abused as children
- 44 percent had sought counseling to help deal with personal relationships

More information about the survey can be obtained by writing the National Lesbian and Gay Health Foundation, PO Box 65472, Washington DC 20035 and asking for the health care source book or *The National Lesbian Health Care Survey: Final Report.*

Gay Youth Suicide

A report by a U.S. Department of Health and Human Services panel stated that gay youths are two to three times more likely to commit suicide than are straight young people. The report, released in August, was the work of the 13-member Task Force on Youth Suicide, appointed in 1986.

The report stressed that homosexuality alone is not a suicide risk factor; the risk is posed by homophobic views in society and the pressure to which this subjects gay youth.

Copies of the 888-page Report of the Secretary's Task Force on Youth Suicide may be obtained for $45.00 from: Superintendent of Documents, U.S. Government Printing Office, Washington DC 20402. **Danni Munson**

LAWS AND LEGISLATION
affecting gay men and lesbians

A number of acts relating to discrimination against people with AIDS were passed by the 100th Congress of the United States before it adjourned on Oct. 22, 1988. The largest appropriation was $1.2 billion for AIDS research, education, and support services. Congress on October 13 passed an omnibus health care bill with many AIDS related provisions. A Fair Housing bill included protections for people with AIDS (PWAs) as did the Civil Rights Restoration Act.

However, there were several defeats of legislation affecting gay Americans. The 100th Congress did not include in the omnibus health care act other protection for PWAs, such as guarantees of confidentiality about AIDS test results. The Senate, threatened with a filibuster by Senator Jesse Helms (R-N.C.), killed a Hate Crimes Statistics bill that had been passed by the House of Representatives. The bill would have required the Department of Justice to gather statistics about crimes against gays and lesbians.

Congress also passed the so-called Armstrong Amendment ordering the District of Columbia to alter its laws forbidding discrimination on the basis of sexual orientation. Congress ordered the district to permit discrimination against gays by religious institutions and to repeal its ban on AIDS testing for insurance purposes. A federal judge in January 1989, however, ruled that Congress could not compel the district to change laws. Congress itself would have to enact that legislation. Nevertheless, gay/lesbian lobbyists pronounced the 100th Congress on the whole a "positive session."

The pro-gay and anti-gay forces took to the battlefield once again after the 101st Congress convened in January 1989. In March 1989, Helms blocked action on a measure to provide $5 million for AZT treatments for needy PWAs. The previously appropriated funds ran out that month. Another ultraconservative, Rep. William Dannemeyer (R-Calif.), succeeded in preventing the launching of a nationwide sexual behavior survey, which scientists claimed was necessary to make predictions about the possible spread of AIDS. (See Health Issues.)

Gay/Lesbian Rights Bill in Congress

A bill that would guarantee civil rights to gay men and lesbians was reintroduced into Congress as it had been each year since the mid-1970s. Gay/lesbian activists reported that the bill is gradually gaining more support. Called the Civil Rights Amendment Act of 1989, the measure was introduced into the House by Ted Weiss (D-N.Y.) and Henry Waxman (D-Calif..), with 63 co-sponsors. It was introduced into the Senate by Alan Cranston (D-Calif.), with eight co-sponsors. More co-sponsors were expected to sign on by the end of the session.

During the 100th Congress, a similar measure eventually gained 73 representatives and 10 senators as co-sponsors. Only one of the co-sponsors was defeated in the November 1988 elections, but not on gay-related issues. (See Politics.)

Bills With Impact on the Gay/Lesbian Community

Lobbyists for AIDS and gay/lesbian concerns focused their attention on bills that could impact on the gay/lesbian community. One was the Americans with Disabilities Act, which would prohibit discrimination against PWAs in accommodations and employment. This measure passed in September 1989. Another measure introduced would protect disabled persons from restrictive, unfit, or abusive guardians. Such issues of guardianship were the focus of Karen Thompson's fight to see her lover Sharon Kowalski, who had suffered brain damage in an auto accident. (See Women's Issues.)

The presence of the gay/lesbian community was felt more strongly than ever during the 101st Congress. There had been only one full-time lobbyist representing gay/lesbian interests in 1987. In 1989, according to a tally

States With Public Employment Protection (laws or executive orders) for gay men and lesbians

State	Date enacted
California	April 1979
Illinois	November 1981
Maryland	N.A.
Michigan	March 1981
Minnesota	November 1986
New Mexico	April 1985
New York	November 1983
Ohio	December 1983
Pennsylvania	September 1978
Rhode Island	August 1985
Washington	December 1985
Wisconsin*	March 1982

* Full equal rights for homsexuals

Source: National Gay and Lesbian Task Force

by *The Washington Blade*, there were at least five full-time gay-concerns lobbyists and three volunteers working the corridors of Congress.

Referenda on Gay/Lesbian Issues

There were a number of AIDS or gay-related referenda on ballots in November 1988. The one that attracted the most attention nationwide was California's Proposition 102, sponsored by conservative Congressman Dannemeyer. It would have required California physicians to report all persons testing positive for the virus that causes AIDS. Proposition 102 was defeated by 66 percent of the voters.

Voters in other states did pass referenda initiatives with negative impact on gay men and lesbians. In Oregon, 53 percent voted to revoke the governor's executive order banning discrimination against gays in public employment and services. The American Civil Liberties Union in June 1989 filed suit challenging the constitutionality of this initiative.

Fifty-seven percent of the voters in Ft. Collins, Colo., rejected a move to include gays in the city's civil rights ordinance, and 56 percent of the voters in St. Paul, Minn., voted against an initiative forbidding the subjection of human rights issues to future referenda.

Local Gay/Lesbian Rights Legislation

An encouraging number of municipalities during the year passed laws prohibiting discrimination on the basis of sexual orientation. The largest was Chicago. The gay/lesbian community there had tried for 15 years to get the Human Rights Ordinance passed. The fight became particularly bitter in 1986, when the ordinance was vehemently opposed by the city's Roman Catholic Archdiocese. But the measure finally passed in December 1988, and as of Feb. 17, 1989, anyone convicted of discriminating against gays in such areas as employment or housing could be fined $500 per day.

Several smaller cities passed measures forbidding discrimination on the basis of sexual orientation: Tacoma, Wash., on May 23, 1989; Alexandria, Va., on Oct. 15, 1988; Oak Park, Ill, on Jun 5, 1989; Muscatine, Ia., on July 6, 1989. Evanston, Ill., also expanded protection for gays and lesbians.

Victories and Defeats at the State Level

The Minnesota Legislature in May 1989 passed a law, effective August 1, that increased penalties for hate crimes committed against gay men and lesbians and other minorities. Activists were hopeful that Massachusetts would soon pass a law protecting gays. The first gay/lesbian rights bill was introduced into the Texas state legislature, and a rights bill was also

However, human rights measures that would have offered protections to gays were defeated in the state legislatures of Connecticut, Illinois, Maine, Rhode Island, and Vermont during the year. An Iowa gay rights law passed the state house but stalled in the senate. The Tennessee legislature amended its "crimes against nature" statute to include only homosexual acts. Tennessee thus became one of seven states that bans homosexual but not heterosexual sodomy. In Washington State, the legislature in May

States With Laws Banning Homosexual Acts Between Consenting Adults

as of Sep. 1, 1989

F=Felony; M=Misdemeanor

Source: National Gay and Lesbian Task Force

State	Penalty
Alabama (M)	Jail term of up to 1 year and/or $2,000 fine
Arizona (M)	Up to 30 days and/or $500
Arkansas (M)	Up to 1 year and/or $1,000
District of Columbia (F)	Up to 10 years and/or $10,000
Florida (M)	Up to 60 days and/or $500
Georgia (F)	Not less than1, up to 20 years
Idaho (F)	Not less than 5 years
Kansas (M)	Up to 6 months and/or $1,000
Kentucky (M)	Up to 1 year and/or $500
Louisiana (F)	Up to 5 years and/or $2,000
Maryland (F)	Up to 10 years and/or $1,000
Massachusetts (F)	Up to 20 years
Michigan (F)	Up to 15 years
Minnesota (M)	Up to 1 year and/or $1,000
Mississippi (F)	Up to 10 years
Missouri (M)	Up to 1 year and/or $1,000
Montana (F)	Up to 10 years and/or $50,000
Nevada (F)	Not less than 1, up to 6 years
North Carolina (F)	Up to 10 years and/or fine
Oklahoma (F)	Up to 10 years
Rhode Island (F)	Not less than 7, up to 20 years
South Carolina (F)	Up to 5 years and at least $500
Tennessee (F)	Not less than 5, up to 15 years
Texas (M)	Fine up to $200
Utah (M)	Up to 6 months and/or $299
Virginia (F)	Not less than 1, up to 5 years or up to 1 year and/or $1,000

1989 deleted sexual orientation from a hate-crimes bill, shocking the local gay/lesbian community, according to the *Seattle Gay News.* In March, a proposed gay rights law for Washington died in committee.

ABA Calls for Gay/Lesbian Protections

The American Bar Association's House of Delegates, meeting in Denver in February 1989, passed a resolution calling on federal, state, and local governments to institute laws forbidding sexual orientation discrimination. The measure passed by a margin of 130 votes and was hailed as a major victory by gay/lesbian activists, who viewed the ABA endorsement as a powerful lobbying tool.

It was the third ABA vote on such a resolution. Previous tries had failed to win sufficient votes in 1983 and 1985.

Gay/Lesbian Partnerships

Significant steps were taken during the year toward legal recognition of gay/lesbian relationships. The New York State Court of Appeals on July 6, 1989, ruled that a gay couple who had lived together for more than 10 years must be considered a family under New York City's rent-control regulations. The ruling blocked an attempted eviction of a man whose lover had died of AIDS. Protection against such evictions "should find its foundation in the reality of family life," wrote the court, not in arbitrary legal or genetic distinctions.

Although the ruling was very narrow, addressing only New York rent-control rules and not Constitutional issues, gay/lesbian activists hailed it as the most significant step to date in gaining legal recognition in the United States for gay/lesbian relationships. Then Mayor Ed Koch soon afterward announced that he would issue an executive order granting bereavement leave to any city employee on the death of a "domestic partner."

Meanwhile, on May 26, 1989, Denmark became the first nation in the world to legalize gay/lesbian marriages. The provision was part of a law that took effect October 1, granting full equal rights to homosexuals.

An attempt to pass a partnership provision in San Francisco met with roadblocks during the year. In May 1989, City Supervisor Harry Britt won approval by the Board of Supervisors for his domestic partnership law. The law allowed gay and heterosexual unmarried couples to register their relationship with the city, receiving in return a certificate and the right to bereavement leave should the partner die. Despite the fact that the law provided few real benefits, the religious right mobilized against it with a petition drive for a voter referendum. In July 1989, they succeeded in having the law suspended until a referendum could be held in November.

(Continued on page 72)

Municipalities With Laws Protecting Lesbians and Gay Men

Key: PE=Public Employment; PA=Public Accommodations; Em=Employment; Ed=Education; RE/H=Real Estate/Housing; C=Credit; UP=Union Practices; II=Intentional Intimidation; NA=Not Available

Municipality	Date Enacted	Type of Protection
Alexandria, Va.	October 1988	PE; PA; Em; Ed; RE/H; C
Alfred, NY	May 1974	PE; PA; Em; Ed; RE/H; C; UP
Amherst, Mass.	May 1976	PE; PA; Em; Ed; RE/H; C; UP
Ann Arbor, Mich.	March 1978	PE; PA; Em; RE/H; C; UP
Aspen, Colo.	November 1977	PE; PA; Em; RE/H
Atlanta, Ga.	March 1986	PE
Austin, Tex.	1976, 1979, 1982	PE; PA; Em; RE/H; C; UP
Baltimore, Md.	May 1988	PE; PA; Em; Ed; RE/H
Berkeley, Calif.	November 1978	PE; Em; Ed; RE/H; C; UP
Boston, Mass.	Jan. & June 1984	PE; PA; Em; Ed; C; UP
Boulder, Colo.	November 1987	PE; PA; Em
Buffalo, NY	April 1984	PE
Burlington Vt.	June 1985	PE; Em
Cambridge, Mass.	September 1984	PE; PA; Em; Ed; RE/H; C; UP
Champaign, Ill.	July 1977	PE; PA; Em; RE/H; C; UP
Chapel Hill, NC	September 1975	PE
Chicago, Ill.	December 1988	PE; PA; Em; C
Columbus, Ohio	January 1979	PE; PA; Em; Ed; RE/H; C
Cupertino, Calif.	February 1975	PE
Davis, Calif.	April 1986	PE; PA; Em; RE/H; C; UP
Dayton, Ohio	October 1984	PE
Denver, Colo.	1983, 1984	PE
Detroit, Mich.	February 1979	PE; PA; Em; Ed; RE/H; C; UP
East Hampton, NY	September 1985	PE; PA; Em
East Lansing, Mich.	December 1986	PE; PA; Em; RE/H; C; UP
Eugene, Ore.	July 1981	II
Evanston, Ill.	1981, 1989	PE; C; NA
Gaithersberg, Md.	June 1987	PE; Em; RE/H; C; UP
Harrisburg, Pa.	March 1983	PE; PA; Em; Ed; RE/H; C; UP
Hartford, Conn.	February 1979	PE
Honolulu, Ha.	March 1981	PE
Houston, Tex.	June 1984	PE
Iowa City, Ia.	April 1979	PE; PA; Em; C; UP
Irvine, Calif.	July 1988	PE; PA; Em; Ed; RE/H; UP
Ithaca, NY	1974; 1984	PE; PA; Em; Ed; RE/H; C; UP
Laguna Beach, Ca.	May 1984	PE; PA; Em; Ed; RE/H; C; UP
Los Angeles, Ca.	June 1979	PE; PA; Em; Ed; RE/H; C; UP
Madison, Wisc.	April 1975	PE; PA; Em; RE/H; C; UP
Malden, Mass.	February 1984	PE; PA; Em; Ed; RE/H; C
Marshall, Minn.	April 1975	PE; PA; Em; RE/H; C
Milwaukee, Wisc.	July 1980	PE
Minneapolis, Minn.	April 1974	PE; PA; Em; Ed; RE/H; C; UP
Mountain View, Ca.	March 1975	PE
Muscatine, Ia.	July 1989	NA

Municipality	Date Enacted	Type of Protection
New York, NY	April 1987	PE; PA; Em; Ed; RE/H; UP
Oakland, Ca.	January 1984	PE; PA; Em; RE/H; C; UP
Oak Park, Ill.	June 1989	NA
Olympia, Wash.	June 1986	PE
Palo Alto, Ca.	NA	Ed
Philadelphia, Pa.	August 1982	PE; PA; Em; RE/H; C; UP
Portland, Ore.	December 1974	PE
Pullman, Wa.	1976, 1981	PE; RE/H; C
Raleigh, NC	January 1988	PE
Rochester, NY	December 1983	PE
Sacramento, Ca.	April 1986	PE; PA; Em; Ed; RE/H; C; UP
Saginaw, Mich.	May 1984	Ed; RE/H
San Francisco, Ca.	1977; 1981	PE; PA; Em; Ed; RE/H; C; UP
Santa Barbara, Ca.	August 1979	PE; Ed
Santa Cruz, Ca.	April 1983	PE
Seattle, Wash.	1973, 1975	PE; Em; RE/H; C; UP
Tacoma, Wash.	May 1989	NA
Troy, NY	January 1979	PE
Tucson, Ariz.	1977, 1981	PE; PA; Em; RE/H; C; UP
Urbana, Ill.	NA	PE; PA; Em; RE/H; C
Washington, D.C.	November 1973	PE; PA; Em; Ed; RE/H; C; UP
W. Hollywood, Ca.	November 1984	PE; PA; Em; Ed; RE/H; C; UP
Yellow Springs, Ohio	July 1975	PE; PA; Em; RE/H; C; UP

Counties With Laws Protecting Lesbians and Gay Men

County	Date Enacted	Type of Protection
Arlington Co., Va.	June 1984	PE
Cayahoga Co., Ohio	August 1986	PE
Clallam Co, Wash.	November 1976	PE
Dane Co., Wisc.	August 1980	PE
Essex Co., NJ	NA	PE
Hennepin Co., Minn.	April 1979	PE
Howard Co., Md.	October 1975	PE; PA; Em; Ed; RE/H; C; UP
Ingham Co., Mich.	June 1978	PE
King Co., Wash.	January 1981	RE/H; C
Minnehaha Co., SD	May 1979	PE
Montgomery Co., Md.	May 1984	PE; Em; RE/H; C; UP
Northampton Co., Pa.	Na	PE
San Mateo Co., Ca.	August 1975	PE; Em; RE/H
Santa Barbara Co., Ca.	October 1982	PE
Santa Cruz Co., Ca.	July 1975	PE
Suffolk Co., NY	March 1988	PE

Source: Prepared with the assistance of the
National Gay and Lesbian Task Force

Conservative Court Trend

The gay/lesbian community watched intently as the Supreme Court of the United States considered issues dealing with personal privacy. The most significant of these cases in 1989 was *Webster vs. Reproductive Health Service*, in which the high court ruled that states have the right to place restrictions on abortions. (See Women's Issues.)

Other rulings that the court made during the 1988-1989 session also seemed to set back hopes for right-to-privacy cases, such as those dealing with homosexual sodomy laws. The Texas Human Rights Foundation in April 1989 filed a law suit challenging the constitutionality of Texas' sodomy law, which makes homosexual acts a crime. However, the challenge was to the Texas state constitution, which is more broadly written than the U.S. Constitution.

"For gay people," summed up Executive Director Tom Stoddard of the Lamdba Legal Defense Fund, "the (Supreme Court) term was disastrous."

Homophobic Judges

A Texas judge drew fire from civil rights groups after telling a Dallas newspaper reporter in December 1988 that he had sentenced a murderer to 30 years instead of life because the victims had been "queers." Judge Jack Hampton allegedly said he regarded "prostitutes and gays at about the same level. I'd be hard put," he said, "to give somebody life for killing a prostitute."

A number of gay and civil rights groups immediately filed complaints with the Texas Commission on Judicial Conduct. Later in December, Hampton apologized for his choice of words, but not for the intent of his remarks. In February 1989, the Commission on Judicial Conduct announced its intent to ask for formal hearings to determine whether Hampton should be removed from the bench.

In Alabama, another judge sparked controversy in December by asking defendants with AIDS not to appear in court. Civil rights groups filed a complaint against Judge Jack Montgomery of Jefferson County, but the complaint was dropped after Montgomery publicly renounced his discriminatory policy in a letter written in February to the local American Civil Liberties Union.

Civil Suit Victories

The first settlement to result from a police raid on a gay bar was announced in Chicago in August 1989. The city and the State of Illinois agreed to pay some $227,000 to 45 men who had been harassed during a 1985 raid on Carol's Speakeasy, a Chicago gay (continued on page 74)

HATE CRIMES

An alarming rise in the number of hate crimes committed against gay men and lesbians was announced by the National Gay and Lesbian Task Force in June 1989. A 40-page NGLTF report "Anti-Gay Violence, Victimization, and Defamation in 1988" reported 7,248 incidents nationwide against homosexuals, 3 percent more than in 1987. The incidents ranged from homicide and assault to verbal abuse and threats of violence. "The vast majority of anti-gay episodes were not reported or counted," said NGLTF's Anti-Violence Project director.

In October 1988, then President Ronald Reagan signed an appropriation bill calling for a hate crimes study by the Department of Justice. The Issues and Practices Study called for was to "highlight existing programs to combat hate crimes and provide guidelines for criminal justice agencies to (1) identify, classify, investigate, and prosecute hate crimes, (2) encourage reporting by hate crime victims, and (3) improve the treatment of hate crime victims."

An exploratory study of hate crimes by the justice department in October 1987 had concluded that "homosexuals are probably the most frequent victims" of hate-motivated incidents.

Anti-gay hate trends on many college campuses also continued during the year. One student, who in March 1989 had sent a hate message through Pennsylvania State University's electronic mail system, was caught. The message, which went out over an international network, called for the extermination of homosexuals. University President Bryce Jordan in April publicly reprimanded the student but said no legal action would be taken because the message was protected by the First Amendment's free speech guarantees.

There were attempts to pass hate crimes legislation. The U.S. House of Representatives again passed the Hate Crimes Statistics Act on July 27, 1989, by a vote of 368 to 7. The bill then went to the Senate where it again faced considerable opposition from Helms, who had succeeded in killing the previous year's hate crimes act.

There was also opposition at the state and local levels. Gays were deleted from a hate crimes bill passed by the Michigan state legislature on Dec. 21, 1988, through the homophobic efforts of state senator Rudy Nichols. The mayor of Columbus, Ohio, asked the city council to remove gay men and lesbians from the list of groups protected by a hate crimes law passed in November 1988. The city council rebuffed the recommendation, and the law went into effect on Dec. 30, 1988.

There were also some local triumphs. San Diego County in late 1988 instituted a Hate Crimes Registry that included gays and lesbians as well as other minorities. An inclusive hate crimes measure was signed into law in St. Louis, Mo., on Feb. 22, 1989. In Washington State, on April 21, 1989, sexual orientation was added to an existing 1981 hate crimes law.

bar. Police allegedly had forced the men to lie on the floor for hours and subjected them to physical and verbal abuse. But none of the men were charged with a crime.

A law suit challenging TWA's frequent flier free-ticket rules resulted in another win for gay men and lesbians in July 1989. A gay man in New York City filed suit in May, charging that TWA's refusal to grant his lover a free companion ticket illegally discriminated against gays. The man had earned the free companion ticket with frequent flier mileage points. But TWA said that only heterosexual spouses and blood relatives were eligible for the award. Nevertheless, TWA changed its policy in July, granting such free tickets to anyone traveling with the original TWA customer. This left only Pan Am and Piedmont, among the major air carriers, with restrictive ticket policies.

The State of Arizona in May said it would allow gays and lesbians to apply for jobs as state police. The action stemmed from a law suit threatened by the National Gay Rights Advocates against the state's practice of subjecting Public Safety Department job applicants to lie detector tests regarding their sexual practices.

In Texas, a lesbian challenged the Dallas Police Department's prohibition against hiring gay people.

Conservative Congressman William Dannemeyer (R-Calif.) lost his libel suit filed in February 1989 against the *Bay Area Reporter*, a gay/lesbian newspaper in the San Francisco area. The suit stemmed from a memo prepared by a research group exploring how Republicans might attack Democrats in the 1988 elections for being "soft on AIDS." The memo, published in the Oct. 8, 1987, issue of the newspaper, said that Dannemeyer was "far too emotional to do any good" and described him as "foaming at the mouth" and "a live grenade." The California Superior Court ruled that the newspaper in printing the memo's contents was protected under California's "fair comment" law and the First Amendment guarantees of freedom of the press.

International Legal Developments

A movement to repeal England's infamous Clause 28, passed by Parliament in early 1988, got underway in 1989. Clause 28 bans the "promotion of homosexuality" by prohibiting government funds being allocated to any organization that supports the legitimacy of a homosexual lifestyle.

Ireland was ordered to repeal legislation outlawing homosexuality. The order came from the European Court of Human Rights on Oct. 26, 1988, and was intended to bring Ireland's laws into line with the rest of the European Community. By May 1989, Dublin had its first gay switchboard, according to *Chicago OUTLINES*. The direct dial number from the United States is: 011-353-2-544855.

Danni Munson

MILITARY MATTERS
affecting gay men and lesbians

Gay men and lesbians continued to face discrimination in the U.S. Armed Forces. They also continued to fight this discrimination in the courts, in Congress, and through appeals to panels of the Department of Defense. Progress was slow, but some limited gains were made.

A Military Campaign Against Women

A series of investigations of suspected lesbians in the U.S. Armed Forces that began in 1987 continued into 1989. There were widespread reports that these investigations were originally instigated by males in the military whose sexual advances had been spurned by women.

A Marine Corps investigation of suspected lesbians at its Parris Island, S.C., base resulted in at least 14 women either being discharged or sentenced to prison terms between June 1988 and June 1989. The military investigators allegedly opened mail, followed the women off the base, and urged women to testify against one another.

In an interview published in Denver's *OUTFRONT* gay/lesbian newspaper, Marine Cpl. Barbara Baum, one of the first to be accused of homosexuality, alleged that her problems at Parris Island began with a serviceman who once had dated a woman Baum was seeing. When the woman rejected his renewed sexual advances, Baum claimed he went to the military authorities and accused both women of being lesbians.

During the resulting investigation, Baum said she was harassed, intimidated, and threatened with a long prison term if she did not cooperate in revealing names of anyone she suspected or knew was a lesbian. She said her military attorney urged her to name names, which she did out of fear and naivety. "I realize now how wrong it was," Baum told the press in March 1989. "I should have taken whatever punishment it was and told them all to drop dead."

Despite her cooperation, Baum was sentenced to one year in the military prison at Quantico, Va. She accused the Marines of reneging on a promise of clemency for cooperation. Baum was released after serving six months of her term, and appealed her discharge to the military high court.

Another Marine imprisoned as a result of the Parris Island investigations, Sgt. Cheryl Jameson, sent a letter to San Francisco's *Coming Up*, stating that military officials offered to "make a deal" in return for her informing on other female Marines. Jameson "flat out refused."

As a result of the informant list they obtained from Baum, the military in

February 1989 brought charges against a female Marine officer. Captain Judy Meade of Camp LeJuene, N.C., was accused of associating with a civilian lesbian, according to documents obtained by ***The Washington Blade***, D.C.'s gay/lesbian newspaper.

Vicky Almquist, director of the Women's Equity Action League Project on Women in the Military said the harassment of Captain Meade was a violation of her Constitutional right to free association. Nevertheless, a Marine Corps board of inquiry recommended in April 1989 that Captain Meade be dismissed with an "Other Than Honorable" discharge. Captain Meade and her attorney fought the discharge recommendation, and in July, a Marine board of review dismissed the charges for lack of evidence. Captain Meade was reassigned to Quantico, where her attorney claimed she suffered repercussions in the form of negative "fitness reports."

A Disproportionate Share of Women

are dismissed from the U.S. Armed Forces for homosexuality each year. While women make up only 10 percent of all U.S. military personnel, they comprise 26 percent of those dismissed for being gay.

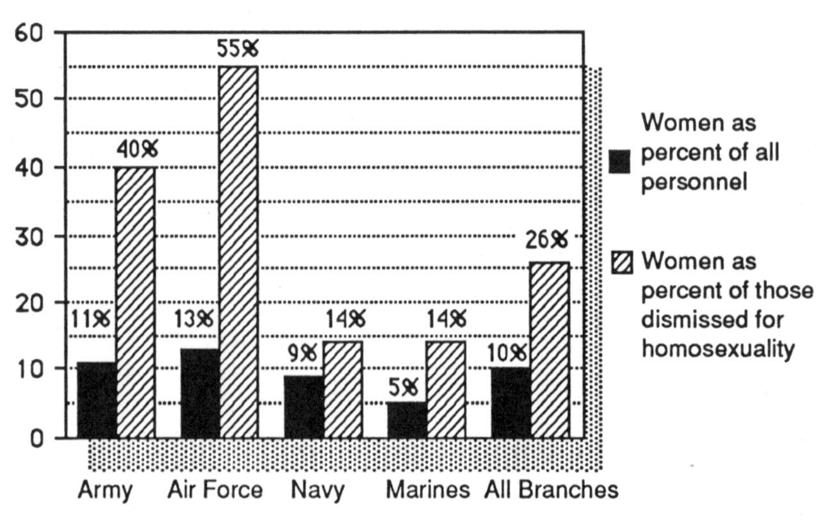

The Navy also went looking for lesbians. In November 1988, a Naval spokesman admitted that 8 of 12 women sailors from the *USS Yellowstone* accused of homosexual conduct were discharged following an investigation. Then in June 1989, Naval officials said that at least two female crew members of the *USS Grapple* were discharged for lesbianism. One of the women charged that this investigation also began after a female crew member turned down the sexual advances of a male crew member. A subsequent attempt in 1989 to discharge a female petty officer aboard the *Grapple* was dismissed for insufficient evidence. Two other cases were sent back for review because of procedural errors.

Investigating the Investigations

Charges of military sexual harassment and the "witch hunts" at Parris Island, Camp LeJuene, and the Norfolk Naval Base attracted attention in Congress. In addition, statistics released by the Pentagon in March revealed that women are discharged from the armed forces on charges of homosexuality much more frequently than are men. Even though women make up about 10 percent of the armed forces, women account for 26 percent of persons discharged for homosexual behavior. Air Force statistics were even more striking: While women account for only 13 percent of Air Force personnel, they make up 55 percent of those dismissed for homosexuality.

Several members of Congress urged the Department of Defense to investigate the dishonorable discharges being brought against women in the military. Defense Department policy, while it does not consider homosexuality compatible with military service, usually provides for an honorable discharge of gays and lesbians.

After hearing testimony from military women and from women's and gay and lesbian advocacy groups, a Defense Department advisory board in April 1989 recommended that training sessions be established to eliminate sexual harassment of females, stop gay-baiting, and discourage unfounded allegations of homosexuality.

Even though activists saw these developments as encouraging first steps, they believed the military had a long way to go before harassment was eliminated. Kathy Gilberd of the National Lawyers Guild Military Law Task Force offered this advice to servicewomen under investigation for lesbian activities: "Say nothing and ask for a lawyer--and start with a civilian lawyer."

Service men were also targets of investigations. A report in the Sept. 8, 1989, *Washington Blade* revealed that hidden cameras had been placed in public washrooms in Japan to catch airmen in homosexual acts.

USS Iowa Explosion

Military investigators raised the specter of homosexual involvement in a tragic explosion in a gun turret aboard the battleship *USS Iowa.* The explosion on April 19, 1989, killed 47 sailors.

The Naval Investigative Service (NIS) in May leaked information that Kendall Truitt, a sailor who survived the blast, may have had a homosexual relationship with Clayton Hartwig, a sailor killed in the blast. Truitt was the beneficiary of a $100,000 insurance policy on Hartwig's life. Truitt, who had recently married, denied the allegations.

The NIS than leaked information indicating they suspected Hartwig of setting off the explosion in an act of suicide after having been spurned in his homosexual advances. NIS investigators claimed another sailor, David Smith, revealed that Hartwig had shown him a timing device for a bomb and had made sexual advances the night before the explosion. Smith denied saying this and accused the NIS of "putting words" in his mouth.

The NIS investigation was widely criticized inside and outside government circles as an attempt to blame a dead man for the explosion. Many irregularities in the handling of ammunition were uncovered aboard the *Iowa.*

In its final, but highly controversial report, the Navy maintained that the explosion was intentionally caused "most likely" by an "unstable" sailor. It did not find proof that Hartwig was a homosexual.

Gay Sergeant Reinstated

A federal appeals court in San Francisco on May 3, 1989, ordered the Army to return openly gay Sgt. Perry Watkins to active duty. Watkins had been drafted into the Army in 1967 despite checking the "homosexual tendencies" box and had repeatedly re-enlisted over the next 14 years even though the Army knew he was gay. Then in 1981 he was denied reenlistment, despite an exemplary record.

In its May ruling, the appeals court cited Perry's Constitutional protection against "double jeopardy." Perry, the court said, had been retained by the Army in the past because the old military rules provided for discharge only if homosexual acts could be proven. The military later changed the rules to allow discharge merely for having a homosexual orientation. The appeals court held that this about face on the rules, in Perry's case, was not fair. The court ruling was very narrow, however, and did not address the broader issues of military discrimination against gays and lesbians, which a three-judge panel of that court had found unconstitutional in February 1988. In October 1988, the February ruling was vacated when the full appeals court agreed to rehear the discrimination case.

Court test of Army's Lesbian Discrimination

A courageous lesbian soldier, Sgt. Miriam Ben-Shalom experienced success and reversal during the year with her suit against the Army's ban on homosexuals. *Ben-Shalom vs. Secretary of the Army* has been in the courts since 1976, when she was discharged for merely stating that she was a lesbian--despite her outstanding service record. A U.S. district court judge in Wisconsin in January 1989 ruled that Ben-Shalom, just because of her sexual orientation, could not be banned from enlisting in the Army Reserves. Such a ban would be unconstitutional. The military policy against any soldier who "evidences homosexual tendencies, desire, or interest, but is without homosexual acts" serves no "legitimate military interest," was the opinion of federal judge Myron Gordon. This was in line with the San Francisco federal appeals court ruling issued in February 1988.

In August 1989, however, a federal appeals court in Chicago upheld the Army's ban on people merely identified as homosexuals, explicitly disagreeing with the San Francisco court of the same ranking. Ben-Shalom's attorney's argued that the Army's rule violates her First Amendment guarantees of free speech. The Chicago federal appeals court dismissed this, stating that while Ben-Shalom's assertion that she is a lesbian "is, in some sense speech, it is also an act of identification. And it is the identity that makes her ineligible for military service...."

The case was likely to be taken to the Supreme Court. However, some activists feared the conservative High Court would rule in favor of the Army, thus setting back the cause of gay/lesbian rights in the military. Gay/lesbian military rights advocates suggested that remedies could better be pursued in Congress through the passage of protective legislation.

Gay Midshipman Sues Government

In January 1989, Joseph Steffan filed suit against the Department of Defense because he had been forced to resign from the Naval Academy at Annapolis, Md., for acknowledging he was gay. The suit, filed by the Lambda Legal Defense and Education Fund, charged this was a violation of his First Amendment free-speech rights and Fifth Amendment rights to due process.

Steffan had a superb record and was one of the top students in his senior class when he learned in March 1987 that the NIS was investigating reports that he was gay. Steffan went to see the Academy commandant and admitted his homosexual orientation. The commandant then convened a discharge board, which forced Steffan to resign just a few weeks before graduation.

Steffan stated that the incident was devastating to himself and his family. His motive for bringing the law suit, he said, was to have the military's ban on gay Americans declared unconstitutional. **Danni Munson**

Gay/Lesbian

ORGANIZATIONS

Organizations dedicated to winning human rights for gay men and lesbians continued to grow during the year. According to *The Washington Blade,* more than 40 new groups formed in the United States just between the 1987 March on Washington and the end of 1988. The greatest proliferation was among chapters of ACT UP (AIDS Coalition to Unleash Power). There were also a number of important changes in some existing gay/lesbian rights organizations.

THE FEDERATION OF GAY GAMES grew out of the old San Francisco Arts & Athletics, Inc., which was expanded and renamed in July 1989. The federation will select the host city and oversee all other matters in regard to future Gay Games. In the past, the gay/lesbian athletic community of the host city sponsored the games and took all responsibility for their organization. (See Special Gay Games Section.)

THE HUMAN RIGHTS CAMPAIGN FUND (HRCF) had become one of the nation's top Political Action Committees by 1989. (See Politics.) Then, the HRCF in June 1989 announced it was dividing its resources and energies into two organizations. The parent group, still known as HRCF, will continue its lobbying efforts on Capitol Hill and its grass-roots organizing activities. The Political Action Committee (PAC), formerly the ninth largest of the approximately 1,115 independent PACs, will now be counted among the 786 "connected" PACs. HRCF also formed the Lesbian Issues and Outreach Project, a political action arm for the lesbian community.

NATIONAL GAY AND LESBIAN TASK FORCE (NGLTF) in June selected lawyer and lesbian activist Urvashi Vaid to replace Jeff Levi as executive director. Levi resigned to work full-time on AIDS issues.

LESBIAN AND GAY FAMILIES PROJECT was founded in May 1989 by the National Gay and Lesbian Task Force and the National Center for Lesbian Rights to work for full recognition of lesbian and gay relationships. Ivy Young, a feminist and black activist, was appointed the director.

NATIONAL CENTER FOR LESBIAN RIGHTS (NCLR) in June 1989 became the new name of the Lesbian Rights Project of Equal Rights Advocates, a public interest law firm based in San Francisco.

ACT UP chapters exist in more than 50 cities in the United States. Organizations modeled on ACT UP have formed in Canadian cities and in London and Paris. ACT UP New York staged the largest AIDS demonstration in March 1989, when 3,000 protesters stormed City Hall to protest inaction on AIDS issues. (For other ACT UP activities, see Health Issues.)

NATIONAL AIDS NETWORK hired AIDS educator Billy S. Jones to head its new minority AIDS program.

THE NAMES PROJECT announced that the October 1989 display of The Quilt in Washington, D.C. will be the last time the full quilt is on display. The more than 12,000 panels have become too expensive to display.

INTERNATIONAL LIONS CLUBS has two mostly gay chapters, the first in San Francisco; the second, chartered in February 1989 in Denver.

INTERNATIONAL LESBIAN AND GAY ASSOCIATION (ILGA) held its 11th World Conference in Vienna, Austria in July, attended by 260 delegates and participants from 33 countries. There was no official delegation from U.S. gay/lesbian organizations, but 21 American activists followed the proceedings. ILGA is making an effort to be officially recognized by the United Nations as a non-governmental organization. The European contact is: RFSL, Box 350, S10124, Stockholm, Sweden.

Waldemar Bojczuk

The International Gay Bowling Organization

is one of the oldest gay/lesbian sports organizations in the United States. Each year since 1981, IGBO has held an annual tournament.

1981--HOUSTON
Singles--Houston, 705
Singles/All Events, NA
Doubles--Houston, 1286
Team--Denver, 3088
Team/All Events--Houston, 5275

1982--DALLAS
Singles--Washington DC, 714
Singles/All Events--Houston, 1982
Doubles--Dallas, 1300
Team--Houston, 2565
Team/All Events: Houston/Phoenix 7358

1983--CHICAGO
Singles--Chicago, 713
Singles/All Events--Chicago, 1988
Doubles--Columbus, OH, 1335
Team--Vancouver, 2643
Team/All Events--Vancouver, 7443

1984--SEATTLE
Singles--Brooklyn, NY, 707
Singles/All Events--Torrence, Calif., 2024
Doubles--Seattle, 1373
Team--Long Beach CA, 2582
Team/All Events--Vancouver, 7448

1985--LOUISVILLE, KY
Singles, San Diego, 749
Singles/All-Events--Atlanta, 2021
Doubles--Dallas, 1374
Team--Toronto, 2563
Team/All Events--Detroit, 7413

1986--LAS VEGAS
Singles--Palm Beach CA, 720
Singles/All Events--Dallas, 2123
Doubles--Anaheim, CA, 1355
Team--New York, 2571
Team/All Events--Omaha, 7500

1987--NEW ORLEANS
Singles--New Orleans, 739
Singles/All Events--New Orleans, 2063
Doubles--Detroit, 1364
Team--New Orleans, 2533
Team/All Events--New York, 7508

1988--WASHINGTON, DC
Singles--Irving, Tex., 765
Singles/All Events--Miami, 2043
Doubles--Carlstadt, NJ, 1419
Team--Houston/Markham, Ill, 2566
Team/All Events--Houston/Markham, Ill., 7361

1989--CINCINNATI
Singles--Tampa, 750
Singles/All Events--Long Beach, 2092
Doubles--Tampa, 1374
Team--San Diego--2615
Team/All Events--LA/Long Beach, 7810

PRIDE GUIDE

Organizations that sponsor local gay/lesbian pride celebrations

International Assn. of Lesbian /Gay Pride Coordinators
c/o Christopher Street West/Los Angeles, 7985 Santa Monica Blvd.
West Hollywood CA 90046 213-656-6553.

ARIZONA
Phoenix Pride Committee
1617 West Village Way,
Tempe AZ 85282.

Old Pueblo Business &
Professional Assn.,
PO Box 44033
Tucson AZ 85745.

CALIFORNIA
Gay & Lesbian Union
411 Eschleman Hall
University of California
Berkeley CA 94720

Long Beach Lesbian & Gay
Pride, Inc.,
2909 E. Anaheim St.
Long Beach CA 90804;
213-439-0696.

Christopher St. West
7985 Santa Monica Blvd.
Suite 109-24
West Hollywood CA 90046
213-656-6553.

Lambda Community Fund
PO Box 163654
Sacramento CA 95816.

San Diego Lambda Pride
PO Box 4191
San Diego CA 92104
619-574-0566 or
619-274-9257.

Lesbian/Gay Freedom Day
Parade & Celebration
584 Castro St. #513
San Francisco CA 94114
415-647-FREE

Gay Pride Celebration
c/o O'Bryan
616 South 12th
San Jose CA 95112

GPW Committee
c/o G & L Action Alliance
PO Box 7293
Santa Cruz CA 95061

COLORADO
Gay Pride Coordinator
PO Drawer E
Denver CO 80218.

CONNECTICUT
Hartford Celebration
c/o J. Foxworth
55 Earle St.
Hartford CT 06120

DELAWARE
Parade Committee
Gay & Lesbian Alliance
214 N. Market St.
Wilmington DE 19801

FLORIDA
South Florida Gay &
Lesbian Pride Committee
PO Box 2048
Ft. Lauderdale FL
305-989-8051.

GEORGIA
Atlanta Gay Center
63 12th St.
Atlanta GA 30309
404-876-5372.

HAWAII
Pride Committee
c/o Gay Community Center
PO Box 3224
Honolulu HI 96801

ILLINOIS
Gay/Lesbian Pride Week
Planning Committee
PO Box 14131
Chicago IL 60614
312-348-8243.

IOWA
Pride Celebration
c/o G. Lynns
320 Hill St.
Dubuque IA 52001
319-583-9018

INDIANA
Justice
PO Box 2387
Indianapolis IN 46206

KANSAS
O. Darrow
6028 SE 45
Tecumseh KS 66542.

Pride Celebration
c/o K. Streips
2126 S.E. Carnahan
Topeka KS 66605

Community Pride Committee
PO Box 3653
Wichita KS 67201
316-267-1852.

KENTUCKY
Gay & Lesbian Hotline
PO Box 992
Louisville KY 40201
502-637-4342.

LOUISIANA
New Orleans Gay Men's Chorus
PO Box 19365
New Orleans LA 70119-9365
504-885-9820.

MAINE
Pride Committee
Box 5122 Sta A
Portland MA 04112

MARYLAND
Baltimore Gay/Lesbian
Community Center
241 W. Chase St.
Baltimore MD 21201
301-837-5445.

MASSACHUSETTS
Boston Pride Celebration
PO Box 8916
Boston MA 02114
617-267-2113

MICHIGAN
Lesbian & Gay Advocates
3116 Michigan Union
University of Michigan
Ann Arbor MI 48109

M.O.H.R.
19641 W. Seven Miles Rd.
Detroit MI 48219.

MISSOURI
MCC of Greater Kansas City
PO Box 10087
Kansas City
MO 64111-0087
816-931-0750

St. Louis Gay Pride Celebration Committee
PO Box 23260
St. Louis MO 63156
314-776-7138; 726-3268.

NEW MEXICO
Common Bond
PO Box 1191
Albuquerque NM 87103
505-266-8041.

NEW YORK
Heritage of Pride
203 Bleecker #11
New York, NY 10012
212-691-1774

OHIO
Columbus Stonewall Union
PO Box 10814
Columbus OH 43201-7814
614-299-7764.

OREGON
Portland Gay/Lesbian Pride
PO Box 6611
Portland OR 97228.

PENNSYLVANIA
MCC Philadelphia
PO Box 8174
Philadelphia PA 19101-8174
215-563-6601.

Gay & Lesbian
Community Center
800 Wood St. #212
Pittsburgh PA 1522
412-243-4522.

SOUTH CAROLINA
Palmetto Gay/Lesbian
Alliance: 803-271-4207

TENNESSEE
Memphis Gay Coalition
PO Box 3038,
Memphis TN 38173
901-726-4299

Tennessee Gay Coalition
PO Box 24181
Nashville TN 37202.

TEXAS
Pride Committee
c/o Political Caucus
Box 822
Austin TX 78767

MCC Dallas
2701 Reagan St.
Dallas TX 75219-3403
214-526-6221

Montrose Activity Center
(HGPW)
PO Box 66684
Houston TX 77266

San Antonio Pride
Committee
3809 Lomita
San Antonio TX 78230.

UTAH
Salt Lake City Gay
Community Council
PO Box 11321
Salt Lake City
UT 84147-0321
801-595-0052.

VIRGINIA
Alexandria Gay
Community Assn.
202-684-0444.

Richmond Gay Alliance
Box 164 Capital Station
Richmond VA 23201
804-358-7090.

WASHINGTON, D.C.
Gay & Lesbian Pride of DC,
c/o T. Adams
4427 39th St.
Brentwood MD 20722
301-783-1828.

WASHINGTON STATE
Seattle Gay News
704 E. Pike
Seattle WA 98122
206-324-4297

Spokane Pride Celebration,
c/o D.W. Schmidt
E 4238 Longfellow #1
Spokane WA 99207.

WISCONSIN
Galvanize
PO Box 1403
Madison WI 53701

Milwaukee Lesbian/Gay
Pride Committee
225 S. Second St.
Milwaukee WI 53204

CANADA
Toronto:
Lesbian and Gay Pride Day
c/o PO Box 1215 Station F
Toronto, Ontario
Canada M4Y 2U8.
Vancouver:
Pride Festival Assn
c/o Dr. Malcolm Crane
1018 Ironwork Passage
Vancouver, B.C.
Canada V6H 3P1

EUROPE
Copenhagen, Denmark
Kurt Nielsen
Godthåbsvej 39, 6th,
Frederiksberg, Denmark 2000.

West Germany:
A. Blumenthal
Jasperallee 32, D-3300
Braunschweig
West Germany
011-49-531-3326-10.

Gay/Lesbian
POLITICS

Gay men and lesbians continued to make strides forward in the political arena. A number of gay Americans were elected or re-elected to public office. Grass-roots activism was high. And polls showed that most voters had a positive attitude toward gay/lesbian civil rights issues.

The Overall Political Climate

The critical event for gay and lesbian politics in the United States during the year was the presidential election in November 1988. During the spring 1988 presidential primary season, all the Democratic candidates for president had voiced support for lesbian and gay civil rights. However, no Republican presidential candidates did so. In addition, 100 openly gay and lesbian delegates attended the Democratic National Convention in Atlanta, while there were none at the Republican National Convention in New Orleans. The nominations of Democrat Michael Dukakis and Republican George Bush continued the contrast between the two parties--Dukakis had a track record of support for gay and lesbian rights, while Bush did not.

The election of Bush in November raised concerns among the community's activists that there would be four more years of failure to enforce civil rights. Of special concern was the impact the Bush election would have on the Supreme Court over the coming decades as Bush was likely to appoint justices of his choice to the high court. Under Ronald Reagan, several conservative justices had been appointed, and early in 1989, this "Reagan Court" began to demonstrate its posture on civil rights. On key civil rights cases the justices limited affirmative action and voted that a state could pass laws restricting or forbidding abortion. Activists feared that the abortion-case ruling could have a far-reaching impact on gay and lesbian privacy rights. (See Laws and Legislation; Women's Issues.)

An analysis by Gay and Lesbian Democrats of America of votes in the 100th Congress revealed that Democrats support gays and lesbians almost twice as often as do Republicans. The votes used in the analysis covered issues ranging from AIDS policy to the Civil Rights Restoration Act. Democrats in the House of Representatives voted in support of pro-gay/lesbian positions more than 86 percent of the time compared with approximately 50 percent pro-gay/lesbian voting for the Republicans. This voting trend continued in the 101st Congress.

At a leadership skills building conference put on from November 18 to 20, 1988, by the National Gay and Lesbian Task Force in Washington, D.C., gay Republicans urged rights leaders not to write off gay Republicans. During a panel discussion, the gay Republicans charged that gay Democrats point out

Openly Gay/Lesbian Elected Officials in Major Public Offices

as of October 1989

Compiled with the assistance of the Hon. John Heilman,council member, City of West Hollywood

NATIONAL OFFICE

U.S. Representative
Barney Frank (D-Mass.)

U.S. Representative
Gerry Studds (D-Mass.)

STATE OFFICE

Minnesota State Representative
Karen Clark

Minnesota State Senator
Alan Spear

Washington State Representative
Calvin Anderson

LOCAL OFFICIALS

CALIFORNIA

Laguna Beach City Council member
Robert Gentry

Sacramento School Board Member
Gary Miller

San Francisco Supervisor
Harry Britt

San Mateo County Supervisor
Tom Nolan

Santa Cruz City Council member
John Laird

Santa Monica City Council member
Judy Abdo

West Hollywood City
Council members John Heilman and Stephen E. Schulte

FLORIDA

Wilton Manors City Council member
John R. Fiore

MAINE

Portland City Councilor-at-large
Barbara A. Wood

MASSACHUSETTS

Boston City Council member
David Scondras

Fall River City Councillor
Steve Camara

MINNESOTA

Minneapolis City Council member
Brian Coyle

MISSOURI

Bunceton City Council member
Gerald Ulrich

NEW YORK

Rochester City Council member-at-large Tim O. Mains

NORTH CAROLINA

Chapel Hill Town Council member
Joe Herzenberg

WISCONSIN

Dane County Supervisors
Tammy S.G. Baldwin, Richard Wagner, Kathleen Nichols

Madison City Alderman
Jim McFarland

ultraconservatives such as Senator Jess Helms (R-N.C.) while ignoring moderate Republicans. During an organized discussion on politics, panelist Mary Jean Collins, of Catholics for Free Choice, challenged the gay Republicans to publicly declare why they had supported George Bush. "I'm sure you voted for him on issues in spite of his stand on gay and lesbian rights," she said, and went on to challenge these "in-spite of" gay Republicans to come out of the closet. United Republicans for Equality and Privacy is urging gay Republicans to approach local and national Republican leaders, according to Gary Bastion, coordinator of UREP.

Gay and Lesbian Elected Officials

Congressional and local elections also impacted on the gay/lesbian community. On a favorable note, none of the Democratic Congressional co-sponsors of the federal gay and lesbian civil rights bill was defeated for re-election. Congress continued to include large Democratic majorities in both houses. Representative Barney Frank (D-Mass.) was overwhelmingly returned to Congress in November 1988 in his first re-election bid since coming out publicly in 1987. (Frank, however, was faced with serious problems in late 1989 over issues involving a male prostitute, who allegedly took advantage of Frank's position to operate a male prostitute ring.) Also re-elected to Congress was another gay representative, Gerry Studds (D-Mass.).

However, a major loss was sustained when Republican Senator Lowell Weicker of Connecticut, who was heavily backed by the Human Rights Campaign Fund, was defeated in his re-election bid. Weicker had been a staunch supporter of gay/lesbian rights and a co-sponsor of the Senate Gay Rights Bill. Reportedly, there were cheers at the Republican election night gala in Washington, D.C., when his defeat was announced.

On the state level, gays and lesbians triumphed in two elections. In Minnesota, Democrat Karen Clark was re-elected to the state house. In his first bid for public office, Democrat Cal Anderson was elected to the Washington State legislature. Democrat Judy Abdo was elected to Santa Monica's city council.

This continued a trend that began in the early 1970s, when the first openly gay candidates for any public office in the United States were elected to the City Council of Ann Arbor, Mich. Their election was followed in 1974 by Elaine Noble's election to the Massachusetts State House of Representatives. She thus became the first openly gay person elected to state-level office. She was followed by Alan Spear, a Minnesota state senator who came out in 1974.

Later in that decade, Harvey Milk became the first openly gay person to win election as a city supervisor in San Francisco, where he served until 1978, when he and Mayor George Moscone were assassinated by a homophobic former supervisor.

Since then, more than 40 openly gay or lesbian people have been elected to various public offices in the United States. Here is a profile of office-holders from the gay/lesbian community in1989:

• As of mid-1989, 31 openly gay Americans held elected office in the United States.

• Of these openly gay elected officials, 28 were Democrats, two were Republicans, and one was a member of the Farmer Labor Alliance.

• The openly gay men and lesbians in elected office came from 11 states: California, Florida, Maine, Massachusetts, Minnesota, Missouri, New Hampshire, New York, North Carolina, Washington State, and Wisconsin.

• California had the most openly gay elected officials, ten, followed by Massachusetts and Wisconsin, each with five.

• The two gay members of the U.S. House of Representatives--Barney Frank and Gerry Studds--are both Democrats from Massachusetts.

• Three gay/lesbian elected officials serve at the state level: Minnesota State Representative Karen Clark, Minnesota State Senator Allan Spear, and Washington State Representative Calvin Anderson.

• No openly gay/lesbian incumbent has ever been defeated at the polls. In 1988, incumbents Clark and Anderson received more than 75 percent of the vote; Frank and Studds received more than 60 percent.

In addition to holding elected office, gays and lesbians have begun to hold other political posts as well. In 1989, there were four openly gay members of the Democratic National Committee--two men and two women. A number of gay men and lesbians also served as appointed public officials on city cabinets, local commissions, and Congressional staffs.

Grass-Roots Activity

Voter registration has become increasingly important in the fight for gay/lesbian rights and political power. In 1988, local gay and lesbian Democratic clubs and PACs organized voter registration drives and get-out-the-vote programs as part of their electoral efforts. Two notable examples of these efforts were in Chicago, Ill., and Washington, D.C.

In Chicago, local gay/lesbian groups registered approximately 15,000 people, more than 33 percent of all newly registered voters in the city. The Chicago voter registration effort showed immediate results--in December, the Chicago City Council passed a landmark gay and lesbian rights law after about 15 years of previously unsuccessful efforts.

In Washington, the Gertrude Stein Democratic Club registered more than 2,500 voters, also 33 percent of the new voters in that city. Washington was again the focus of grass-roots organizing efforts in December 1988, when the U.S. Congress threatened to cut off funds for the city if the council did not repeal its strict gay anti-discrimination law.

In New York City, David N. Dinkins, heavily supported by the gay/lesbian community, won the Democratic mayoral primary in September, defeating Ed Koch. Both candidates had actively courted the gay/lesbian vote.

Voter Attitudes Toward Gays

More information became available during the year about voter attitudes on

Where the Human Rights Campaign Fund Stood Among the Major PACs at the end of 1988 in Funds Raised

Independent PACs	Funds raised
1. National Security PAC	$10,277,264
2. National Committee to Preserve Social Security	$4,506,792
3. Auto Dealers & Drivers for Free Trade	$4,471,696
4. National Congressional Club (Helms)	$4,150,677
5. American Citizens for Political Action	$3,879,687
6. Campaign America	$3,781,393
7. Voter Guide '88	$3,359,300
8. National PAC	$2,435,240
9. Human Rights Campaign Fund	**$2,292,137**
10. National Committee for an Effective Congress	$2,247,769
11. National Conservative PAC	$2,205,154
12. RUFF PAC	$2,124,719
13. Fund for America's Future	$1,860,986
14. Congressional Majority Committee	$1,733,668
15. National Right to Life PAC	$1,660,936

Source: *The Washington Blade*, 1989

gay/lesbian issues through a 1989 poll by the *San Francisco Examiner*. Of 4,148 people surveyed, 400 identified themselves as gay. Of the 3,748 non-gay respondents, 80 percent felt it was discriminatory to deny someone a job because of their sexual orientation. Only 9 percent of non-gay respondents felt homosexuality should be illegal, while 73 percent believed it should not. Almost three-fourths of the straights surveyed said they would vote for a gay or lesbian candidate with whom they agreed politically.

Of those claiming to be gay, 51 percent described themselves as Democrats; 19 percent, as Republicans. In terms of outlook and attitudes, 29 percent of the gays polled said they were very liberal; 41 percent, liberal; 22 percent, moderate, and 7 percent, conservative. Of the straights surveyed by the *Examiner*, only 6 percent said they were very liberal; and 31 percent, conservative. (See Event of the Year for more survey data and information on how to order reprints of the *Examiner's* 16-part series, "Gay in America.")

Politics Since Stonewall

June 1989 marked the 20th Anniversary of New York City's Stonewall riots and the birth of the modern gay/lesbian rights movement. Since then, gay/lesbian activists have made significant gains in winning and protecting civil rights for gay men and lesbians and in the political arena as a whole.

In the 1968 presidential election, just six months before Stonewall, no presidential candidate even mentioned gay rights. No city or state had laws affirming and protecting gay/lesbian rights. No elected officials were openly gay.

In 1989, gay and lesbian rights issues were actively on the agenda of American politics. And with continued work, we can look forward to full civil rights protection and participation in the political process when we celebrate the 40th Anniversary of Stonewall in 2009.

Christine Riddiough
Executive Director, Gay and Lesbian Democrats of America

Gay and Lesbian Democratic Clubs in America

(Alphabetically by state)

ALABAMA

Privacy Rights Organization PAC
PO Box 55913
Birmingham AL 35205

ARIZONA

Democratic Caucus/ Arizona Gay/Lesbian Task Force
3637 E. Monterosa #12
Phoenix AZ 85018

Arizona Gay/Lesbian Democrats
9260 E. Summer Trail
Tucson AZ 85749

CALIFORNIA

Harvey Milk Lesbian/Gay Democratic Club
Los Angeles CA 90026

Stonewall Democratic Club
PO Box 38812
Los Angeles CA 90038

California Assn. of Lesbian/Gay Democratic Clubs
3212 Silverado Dr.
Los Angeles CA 90039

West Hollywood Democratic Club
7548 Lexington Ave.
W. Hollywood CA 90046

West Hollywood Democratic Club
PO Box 691005
W. Hollywood CA 90069

Lambda Democratic Club
PO Box 14454
Long Beach CA 90803

San Diego Democratic Club
PO Box 80193
San Diego CA 92138

Eleanor Roosevelt Democratic Club
3941B Bristol St. #420
Santa Ana CA 92704

Alice B. Toklas Democratic Club
PO Box 11316
San Francisco CA 94101

Harvey Milk Democratic Club
PO Box 33915
San Diego CA 92103

Stonewall Lesbian/Gay Democratic Club
473 Corbett Ave.
San Francisco CA 94114

Harvey Milk Lesbian//Gay Democratic Club
PO Box 14368
San Francisco CA 94114

Lesbian/Gay Caucus California Democratic Party
561 28th St.
San Francisco CA 94131

Gay & Lesbian Area Democrats
PO Box 139
Concord CA 94522

East Bay Lesbian/Gay Democratic Club
PO Box 443
Berkeley CA 94701

Freedom Democratic Caucus
1214 King St.
Santa Cruz CA 95060

Susan B. Anthony Democratic Club
705 S. 11th
San Jose CA 95112

Gay & Lesbian Democratic Club
PO Box 6201
Santa Rosa CA 95406

River City Democratic Club
PO Box 161958
Sacramento CA 95816

COLORADO

Colorado LGDC
1029 E. 8th Ave. #606
Denver CO 80218

DISTRICT OF COLUMBIA

Gertrude Stein Democratic Club
PO Box 21067
Washington DC 20009

DELAWARE

Roosevelt-Milk Democratic Club
608 W. 28th St.
Wilmington DE 19802

FLORIDA

Florida Task Force
411 Chapel Dr. #226
Tallahassee FL 32304

Central Florida Gay/Lesbian Democrats c/o Ford
1505 Shady Acres Lane
Apopka FL 32703

Olde Towne Democratic Club
PO Box 1708
Key West FL 33040

Dan Bradley Democratic Club
3775 Poinciana Ave.
Miami FL 33133

Dade County Coalition for Human Rights
3775 Poinciana Ave.
Miami FL 33133

Dolphin Democratic Club
PO Box 39502
Ft. Lauderdale FL 33339-9502

Atlantic Coast Democratic Club
618 NW 13th St. #31
Boca Ratan FL 33486

Bay Area Rights Council
14450 Bruce Downs Blvd.
Tampa FL 33613

GEORGIA

LEGAL
PO Box 54105
Atlanta GA 30308-0105

HAWAII
Hawaii Democrats for Gay/ Lesbian Concerns
Box 8061
Honolulu HI 96830

IOWA
Lesbian/Gay Democratic Caucus of Story County
708 Douglas
Ames IA 50010

Des Moines Gay/Lesbian Democratic Club
3500 Kingman Blvd.
Des Moines IA 50311

Gay & Lesbian Democrats of Iowa
PO Box 611
Iowa City IA 52244

ILLINOIS
LGPDO
3225 N. Sheffield
Chicago IL 60657

Prairie State Democratic Club
c/o Annex, 3160 N. Clark
Chicago IL 60657

KENTUCKY
Gay/Lesbian Democrats of Kentucky
PO Box 187
Lexington KY 40584

MASSACHUSETTS
Bay Sate Lesbian/Gay Democratic Club
PO Box 6191 JFK Sta.
Boston MA 02114

MARYLAND
Montgomery County Gay Democrats
7608 Quincewood
Rockville MD 20855

Baltimore Lesbian/Gay Democratic Club
c/o Walker
2277 Park Hill
Baltimore MD 21211

MAINE
Lesbian & Gay Democratic Club of Maine
RFD #1, Box 697
Monmouth ME 04259

MINNESOTA
Lesbian/Gay Caucus MN DFL
2414 Stevens Ave. S.
Minneapolis MN 55404

MISSOURI
Lesbian/Gay Democrats of Missouri
2053 Alfred St.
St. Louis MO 63110

MISSISSIPPI
Mississippi Lesbian/Gay Democratic Caucus
PO Box 8342
Jackson MS 39204

NEW HAMPSHIRE
Lesbian/Gay Democrats of New Hampshire
9 Christopher Rd.
Merrimack NH 03054

NEW MEXICO
New Mexico Lesbian/Gay Political Alliance
PO Box 25191
Albuquerque NM 87125

NEW YORK STATE
Stonewall Democratic Club
PO Box 1750 Old Chelsea Sta
New York NY 10011

Caucus of Lesbian/Gay Dist. Leaders
80 Eighth Ave.
New York NY 10011

Gay/Lesbian Independent Democrats
PO Box 7241
New York NY 10150

Bronx Gay/Lesbian Independent Democrats
PO Box 736, Jerome Ave. Sta.
Bronx NY 10468

Lambda Independent Democrats
44 5th Ave. #151
Brooklyn NY 11217

Eleanor Roosevelt Democratic Club
PO Box 2180
Albany NY 12220-2180

Rochester Lesbian & Gay Political Caucus
713 Monroe Ave.
Rochester NY 14607

NORTH CAROLINA
Lesbian/Gay Democrats of North Carolina
PO Box 307
Chapel Hill NC 27514

OREGON
Lesbian Gay Caucus of the Oregon Democratic Party
1703 SW Montgomery Dr.
Portland OR 97201

PENNSYLVANIA
Philadelphia Equal Rights Coalition
4519 Osage
Philadelphia PA 19143

TEXAS
Lesbian/Gay Democrats of Texas
201 Peach St.
Denton TX 76201

GLDA Houston
PO Box 66275
Houston TX 77266

Houston Gay Political Caucus
Box 3624
Houston TX 77266

UTAH
Lesbian & Gay Democrats of Utah
PO Box 11213
Salt Lake City UT 84147

VERMONT
Lesbian/Gay Caucus of the Vermont Democratic Party
46 Crowley St.
Burlington VT 05401

WASHINGTON STATE
Gay Democrats of Greater Seattle
PO Box 1975
Seattle WA 98111

WISCONSIN
Lesbian/Gay Caucus of the Wisconsin Democratic Party
Madison WI 53704

RELIGION

There were significant gains and significant losses in efforts to educate religious organizations about gay/lesbian issues and gain recognition of homosexuality as a valid, moral lifestyle. The Roman Catholic Church continued its campaign to eliminate Dignity, the organization of gay/lesbian Catholics. But the Episcopal Church and the United Church of Canada moved toward more enlightened viewpoints. Meanwhile, the Universal Fellowship of Metropolitan Community Churches continued to act as a haven for those unable to find one in the mainline Christian churches. And, to facilitate communications, the first ecumenical gay/lesbian newspaper began publishing during the year.

Jewish Education Fund

A fund to help print educational material about gay Jews was set up in December 1988 by the World Congress of Gay and Lesbian Jewish Organizations. The fund was named for Rabbi Hershel J. Matt, who attempted to educate Jewish leaders about homophobia in the Jewish community. Establishment of the fund was announced on December 13, the first anniversary of his death. Tax deductible contributions may be sent to: Rabbi Hershel J. Matt Education Fund, The World Congress of Gay and Lesbian Jewish Organizations, PO Box 18961, Washington DC 20036.

Ordination Issues

The United Church of Canada in August 1988 agreed to ordain practicing homosexuals as ministers. The resolution was approved by the church's General Council meeting in Vancouver, B.C. With 863,000 members, the United Church is Canada's largest Protestant denomination. The ordination of gays and lesbians did not set well, however, with many church members. Some observers feared the issue might split the church.

Ordination was also a concern for Lutherans Concerned. At the sixth biennial convention of the Lutheran gay/lesbian concerns group in Toronto in 1988, they took up the issue of the double standard for gay/lesbian Lutheran clergy, according to a report in *The Second Stone*. The Lutheran Church requires gay men and lesbian clergy to be celibate, but has no such rule for straight clergy. Lutherans Concerned issued "A Call for Repentance" to the Evangelical Lutheran bishops, pointing out ways that the church discriminates against gay/lesbian Christians.

The Eastern North Dakota Synod in 1989 passed (continued on page 94)

UNIVERSAL FELLOWSHIP OF METROPOLITAN COMMUNITY CHURCHES

by Rev. Sandi Robinson
Director of Ecumenical Ministry
UFMCC

UFMCC, a Christian denomination with a special outreach to the gay and lesbian community, held its 14th General Conference in July 1989 in St Paul, Minn. The conference theme, "Good News for All People," provided grist for sermons, workshops, and seminars that revitalized the denomination's understanding of ministry in a hostile world.

The denomination's AIDS ministry was strengthened with the creation of the post of field director of AIDS ministry, and its ecumenical vision broadened.

Among the speakers and workshop presenters were: Dr. Carter Heyward, feminist theologian; Dr. Thomas Hanks, liberation theologian; Dr. Virginia Mollencott, author and lecturer; and Camille Bell, founder of SOLACE, an Atlanta-based organization. Another speaker, Dr. John Boswell, was awarded the UFMCC 1989 Human Rights Award. Dr. Boswell, a Yale University history professor, authored "Christianity, Social Tolerance and Homosexuality."

The World Council of Church's invited UFMCC's Director of Ecumenical Ministry, Rev. Sandra Robinson, one of 40 observers from the United States, to participate in its Conference on Mission and Evangelism in May 1989 in San Antonio, Tex. UFMCC had been invited into participation at the Consultation on Church Union General Assembly in New Orleans in December 1988.

This ecumenical witness of UFMCC in the world has strengthened the denomination's impact on the international Christian landscape, especially since UFMCC made application in 1981 for membership in the National Council of Churches in the USA. Although UFMCC was declared eligible for membership, the application was not voted on. Instead, a process of conversation and dialogue was developed. These included consultations on Biblical Interpretation, Human Sexuality, and Ecclesiology.

The Department of People of Color in UFMCC held its biennial Leadership Conference in November 1988 at Grailville, Ohio. Subsequently, the Department's Minority AIDS Ministry coordinator, Rick Espinoza traveled to Nicaragua; Rev. Hong Tan traveled to China during the mid-1989 protests and resulting massacre; and the UFMCC Elders established the Fund for Overcoming Racism. A trip to South Africa was being planned during late 1989.

UFMCC's seminary, Samaritan College, in September 1988 initiated its first secular class in the area of Lesbian Studies. The seminary's developing College of Human Service eventually will also include Gay Male Studies, Community Organization and Administration, Counseling and Social Work.

Universal Fellowship of Metropolitan Community Churches Districts Worldwide

UNITED STATES

Great Lakes District
PO Box 5757
Dayton OH 45405-0757
513-277-8815

Gulf Lower Atlantic District
PO Box 401
Montgomery AL 36101
205-264-7887

Mid-Central District
1520 Sieben
Topeka KS 66611
913-354-8451

Mid-Atlantic District
PO Box 686
Germantown MD 20874
301-540-4204

Northeast District
PO Box 27
Scarborough NY 10510
914-941-1145

Northwest District
PO Box 5795
Sacramento CA 95817
916-448-3106

South Central District
PO Box 262822
Houston TX 77207-2822
713-649-5645

Southeast District
625 Jefferson Ave. N.
Sarasota FL 34237
813-334-4443

Southwest District
33881 Manta Court
Laguna Niguel CA 92677-3823
714-240-1364

CANADA

Western Canada
PO Box 245
Maple Ridge
British Columbia V2X 7G1
604-462-9813

Eastern Canada
1502-10 Walmer Rd.
Toronto, Ontario M5R 2W4
416-924-3229

OTHER COUNTRIES

Australia
25/21 South Terrace
Adelaide, So. Australia 5000
(08) 231-3870

European/North Sea
PO Box 59
Wolverhampton WV4 5TR
ENGLAND
(0902) 341450

World Church Extension
Rev. Elder Jean White
2A Sistova Rd., Balham
London, England SW12 9QT
(01) 675-676-1110

a resolution affirming gays and lesbians, making it the first synod to welcome gay Lutherans to its churches.

Dignity Problems

Dignity continued to suffer from the Roman Catholic Church's demand that members return to regular parishes, renounce the Dignity name, and give up the assertion that homosexuality is compatible with a Christian lifestyle. The eviction of Dignity chapters from meeting space in parish churches was completed during the year when San Francisco Dignity was evicted from the church where it had met for 15 years. The last Dignity mass was held there on Dec. 18, 1988.

The evictions began in 1986, after Cardinal Josef Ratzinger denounced gays as "intrinsically disordered." The Vatican then also began to harden its line against homosexuals. As a result, Dignity chapters have had to seek space for masses and meetings in Protestant churches and other places.

The pressure from Catholic bishops reportedly frightened many conservative gays and lesbians, who left Dignity and returned to their parish churches. It also has caused splits in some chapters. In New York, for example, Dignity Big Apple is the more conservative group, following most of the basic church doctrines; Dignity/New York is more radical, calling for many reforms including ordination of women. In addition, Dignity chapters have begun to take on more social issues.

The changes have made Dignity stronger, according to Executive Director Jim Bussen. "We're changing our religious character, not losing it," he told a reporter for *The Second Stone*. He added that "we still consider ourselves Roman Catholic."

National Gay/Lesbian Ecumenical Newspaper Debuts

A new resource for gay men and lesbians interested in following religious issues began publication in late 1988. *The Second Stone* appeared on the scene with its November/December 1988 issue.

The newspaper is published every two months and covers a broad range of issues involving all denominations. Subscriptions are $12.00 for six issues (one year).

Letters, news, and subscription requestss should be mailed to:

The Second Stone
P.O. Box 8340
New Orleans LA 70182

Bussen received the Paul R. Goldman Award from the Chicago Interfaith Congress in July 1989 for his tireless work in trying to educate American Catholic Bishops about gay and lesbian concerns.

AIDS and the Church

There were varied responses to the AIDS crisis by different denominations. The American Baptist General Board issued a policy statement emphasizing that AIDS is not a punishment from God and called upon their members to "work to eliminate discrimination in all sectors of life against those thought to have the AIDS virus."

The Southern Baptists, on the other hand, refused to distribute the U.S. Surgeon General's educational material about AIDS. They did not think the Surgeon Generals's report adequately addressed "morality" issues.

Metropolitan Community Churches at its General Conference in St. Paul, Minn., in July established a full-time field director of AIDS ministry, Rev. Steve Pieters. Rev. Pieters, a long-time survivor of the AIDS infection, wrote a new pamphlet, "Spiritual Strength for Survival."

Woman Episcopal Bishop and Gay/Lesbian Rights

The first female Bishop of the Episcopal Church, Rev. Barbara C. Harris, came out strongly in favor of gay/lesbian rights. Bishop Harris was consecrated in that post on Feb. 11, 1989. Activists involved with Integrity, the association of gay/lesbian Episcopalians, were very pleased with Harris's election and expected her to have a positive impact on church policy.

Meanwhile, Rev. Richard F. Grein, the only candidate labeled "unacceptable" by Integrity, was elected Bishop of New York. Grein had publicly opposed openly gay Episcopalian clergy. However, Grein's attitude appeared to be softening after he took up the duties of the post (but had not yet been consecrated) in June 1989. He even presided at an Integrity service in a Greenwich Village Church.

News From Other Denominations.

The Restoration Church of Jesus Christ, which serves gay/lesbian Mormons in Salt Lake City, ordained a lesbian as Presiding Bishop, the first such appointment in Mormon history.

A support group for former Jehovah's Witnesses who are gay or lesbian was formed during the year to help kindred spirits deal with issues of sexuality and excommunication. They can be reached at: Common Bond, PO Box 405, Ellwood City, PA 16117. **Danni Munson**

Gay/Lesbian Jewish Organizations in North America

For Jewish Groups in other countries, contact: World Congress of Gay/Lesbian Jewish Organizations, PO Box 881272, San Francisco CA 94188

CANADA

Toronto GSH c/o Wiseberg
15 Arrowstock Rd.
Willowdale, Ontario
CANADA

Yakhdav c/o Brody
3617 Marlowe Ave.
Montreal, Quebec
CANADA H4A 3L8

Chutzpah
770 Huntley St. #1823
Toronto, Ontario
CANADA M4Y 2P3

The Jewish Gay/Lesbian Group
PO Box 3556
Vancouver B.C.
CANADA V6B 3Y6

UNITED STATES

Mishpochet Am
PO Box 39127
Phoenix AZ 85069

Gay Gezundt
PO Box 41684
Tucson AZ 85717

Cong. Beth Chayim Chadashim
6000 W. Pico Blvd.
Los Angeles CA 90035

Yachad
PO Box 3027
San Diego CA 92103

Cong. Sha'ar Zahav
220 Danvers at Caselli
San Francisco CA 94114

Tikvat Shalom
PO Box 6694
Denver CO 80206

Am Segulah
PO Box 54
Hartford CT 06141-0554

Beth Mishpacha
PO Box 1410
Washington DC 20013

Cong. Etz Chaim/Metro Comm. Syng.
19094 W. Dixie Hwy
N. Miami Beach FL 33180

Bet Haverim
PO Box 54947
Atlanta GA 30308-0947

Or Chadash
656 W. Barry
Chicago IL 60657

Havurot Achayot
PO Box 14066
Chicago ILL 60614

Lambda Chai/New Orleans
PO Box 2223
New Orleans LA 70176

Jewish Lesbian Daughters of Holocaust Survivors
PO Box 6194
Boston MA 02114

Am Tikva
PO Box 11
Cambridge MA 02238

Adath Rayoot c/o Gay Community Center
PO Box 22575
Baltimore MD 21203

Lambda Chai
PO Box 2441
Farmington Hill MI 48018

Simcha (Detroit)
PO Box 652
Southfield MI 48037

Beyt G'Vurah
PO Box 8503
Minneapolis MN 55408

L'Cha Dodi
PO Box 32003
Kansas City MO 64111

Cong. Beth Simchat Tora
PO Box 1270 G.P.O.
New York NY 10016

Zionist Union of Gays & Lesbians, NY c/o CBST
PO Box 1270 G.P.O.
New York NY 10116

Beth Chai
PO Box 451
Farmingdale NY 11735

Nayim
PO Box 18053
Rochester NY 14618

Chevrie Tikva
PO Box 18120
Cleveland OH 44118-0120

Baleboosteh
PO Box 11134
Eugene OR 97440

Daughters of Lillith c/o Yacknin
2013 Sampson St.
Pittsburgh PA 15221

Bet Tikvah c/o Persad Center
5100 Pennsylvannia Ave.
Pittsburgh PA 15224

Cong. Beth Ahava
PO Box 7566
Philadelphia PA 19100

Beth El Binah
PO Box 64460
Dallas TX 75206

Aytz Chayim
5800 Lumberdale Rd. #2
Houston TX 77092

Banot Uvanim
PO Box 11621
Norfolk VA 23517

Cong. Tikvah Chadashah
PO Box 2731
Seattle WA 98111-2731

Hava Machmias
4944 N. Newhall
Milwaukee WI 53217

Women's Issues

Lesbians confronted sexual harassment and discrimination on a number of fronts during the year, from military "witch hunts" to the threat of all women losing the right to chose abortion (See Military Matters). Across the country, however, lesbians worked toward establishing a national agenda of concerns.

National Conferences; National Agenda

More than 1,000 lesbians gathered in San Diego from October 7 through 10, 1988, for the National Lesbian Rights Conference sponsored by the National Organization for Women. The theme of the conference "Power Through Action," focused on how to get and use political power. The stated purpose of the conference was to help develop a national agenda of lesbian concerns. Speakers at the conference stressed lesbian strength through lesbian diversity--economic, ethnic, and racial. However, not all participants were satisfied that this diversity was directed toward concrete, unified goals. Many even questioned NOW's commitment to lesbians, especially lesbians of color.

Dissatisfaction with NOW's conference gave rise to renewed calls for a national lesbian agenda for social, economic, and political change, developed by and for lesbians. The idea originally grew out of the 1987 March on Washington. Six regional meetings and two national planning meetings were held in preparation for the conference.

The first National Lesbian Planning Meeting took place in Raleigh-Durham, N.C., March 4-5, 1989, attended by 175 lesbians. Although the meeting became bogged down in debates, a site was chosen: Atlanta, Ga. At the next national meeting, in Portland in July 1989, a date for the national lesbian agenda conference was set: April 25 to 28, 1991.

NOW's National Conference, held in Cincinnati from July 21-23, 1989, passed a lesbian rights resolution that specifically addressed issues of lesbians of color. "NOW recognizes that lesbians of color have additional issues facing them, namely racism, cultural diversity, classism, and economic conditions," the resolution stated. In addition, an updated NOW Lesbian Rights Resources Kit will have a Lesbians of Color section. NOW also called for an "Expanded Bill of Rights for the 21st Century" to be added to the U.S. Constitution, including freedom from discrimination on the basis of sexual orientation.

Many Lesbians Support Pro-Choice March

The threat to a woman's right to chose abortion brought hundreds of thousands of women from all walks of life together in Washington, D.C., on April 9, 1989, for a massive March on Washington for Women's Equality and Women's Lives. Many lesbians lent their support to this issue, and gay and lesbian activists were much in evidence during the pro-choice march.

High levels of fear and concern that the right to choose might be denied women prevailed during 1988 and 1989 as anti-choice factions stepped up lobbying pressure to have the famous *Roe vs. Wade* Supreme Court decision--which allowed for legalized abortion--overturned. They also lobbied for an anti-abortion Amendment to the U.S. Constitution.

However, neither side could claim victory when the Supreme Court on July 3, 1989, let stand a Missouri law restricting abortion in *Webster vs. Reproductive Health Services.* Although the court's ruling did not overturn *Roe vs. Wade,* it meant that each state was free to restrict or outlaw abortion. This, in turn, meant that the pro-choice/anti-choice battle would have to be fought state by state.

Sharon Kowalski Sets Out Toward Home

The long fight by Karen Thompson to see her lover, Sharon Kowalski, achieved victory in 1989. Kowalski, who had suffered brain damage that left her a paraplegic in an auto accident in November 1983, had been under the guardianship of her father. He denied his daughter was a lesbian and refused to allow Thompson to see her.

The Thompson/Kowalski story became a cause célèbre in the gay/lesbian community. In 1985, Sharon's father was awarded legal guardianship and had Sharon isolated in a nursing home, where she received no rehabilitative therapy.

Until the accident, both Thompson and Kowalski led very closeted lives in Minnesota. Thompson "came out" over the issue, fighting for custody of Kowalski in the courts of law and of public opinion. Her book *Why Sharon Kowalski Can't Come Home,* documents homophobia and paternalism toward the handicapped in our society.

The story began to turn around in December 1988, when a Minnesota judge ruled that Kowalski should be removed from the nursing home and placed in a rehabilitation facility in Duluth. The move took place on Jan. 17, 1989. Doctors, not Sharon's father, then determined who could visit. On Feb. 3, 1989, Thompson saw her lover for the first time since August 1985. On May 18, Kowalski was moved to a long-term rehabilitative care facility in Minneapolis, about an hour's drive from Thompson's home.

While this episode in the lives of Thompson and Kowalski seemed headed for resolution, the larger issues of legal rights for committed same-sex couples remained open. "Our voices must be heard in large enough numbers," wrote Thompson in her book, "that what we have to say cannot be discounted, cannot be ignored." Otherwise "...the question tomorrow might be, why can't you come home."

Danni Munson

Gay/Lesbian

EVENTS

of

1990

For Index of Events by type,
please refer to the back of the book

Sun	Mon	Tues	Wed	Thur	Fri	Sat
	1	2	3	4	5	6
7	8	9	10	11	12	13
14	15	16	17	18	19	20
21	22	23	24	25	26	27
28	29	30	31			

January 1

Special New Year's Resort Weekend in the Saugatuck/Douglas area of Michigan at the Douglas Dunes resort motel. Write: Douglas Dunes, PO Box 369, Douglas MI 49406; call: 616-857-1401.

New Year's at Winter Park, a holiday ski outing for gays and lesbians in Colorado. Write: Colorado Outdoor & Ski Assn., PO Box 18598, Denver CO ; call: 303-470-9658.

Brunch dance in Seattle at Timberline, the city's premier Western dance bar. Write: Puddletown Squares, PO Box 20671, Seattle WA 98102; call: 206-324-8786.

January 7

Spiritual Program of Dignity/Central Indiana begins and continues on the first Suday of the month throughout the year. Second Sundays are Pitch-In Dinners and Business meetings. Third, fourth, and Fifth Sundays are Social or Educational Programs. Write: Dignity/Central Indiana, PO Box 431, Indianapolis IN 46206.

January 12

Square Dance Fly-In in Phoenix, cohosted by the Desert Valley Squares, the Sunburst Dancers, and the Arizona Gay Rodeo Assn. Write: Desert Valley Squares, PO Box 34615, Phoenix AZ 85067; call: 602-978-3273

Road Runner Regional Rodeo begins in Phoenix and continues through January 14, with events such as wild bull riding, calf roping, and steer decorating. For details, write Arizona Gay Rodeo Assn., PO Box 16363, Phoenix AZ 85011.

M.O.I.S.T. Bowling Tournament in Miami, Fla., begins and continues through January 15. Call: 305-252-1455.

January 13

S.W.I.F.T. Bowling Tournament at Seal Beach, Calif., begins and continues through Janaury 14. Call: 213-437-5253.

Women's Ski Trip through January 15 to Diamond Head Ski Chalet in Washington State, for intermediate backcountry skiers to a ski hut in the Coast Range of Canada. Write: Woodswomen, 25 W. Diamond Lake Rd., Minneapolis MN 55419; phone: 612-822-3809.

January 17

AIDS and Mental Health Educational Conference for professional caregivers begins in Berkeley, Calif., and continues through January 19, covering legal issues for mental health professionals working with HIV-infected and at-risk groups. Write: AIDS Health Project, 1855 Folsom St., Suite 506, San Francisco CA 94103; call: 415-476-6430.

January 19

Skiing Weekend at Mammoth Mountain leaves aboard charter bus from Long Beach for two nights at Meadowridge Condos. Write: The Gay and Lesbian Center of Long Beach, 2017 E. 4th St., Long Beach CA 90814; call: 213-434-4455.

January 20

Women's Rafting Day Trip on Washington's Skagit River to view eagles and other wildlife. No rafting experience necessary for 10 mile stretch of calm water. All women welcome, not limited to lesbians. Write: Womantrek, 1411 E. Olive Way, PO Box 20643, Seattle WA 98102; call: 206-325-4772.

Annual Snow Run for Antique Auto Buffs, through January 21, sponsored by the Northwest Scenic Cruisers of Oregon, 206-254-1995.

Gay/Lesbian Ski Week in Aspen, Colo., when the whole town turns gay. For information and accommodations see your gay/lesbian travel agent. For the closest one, call the International Gay Travel Association:

303-467-7117 or contact the Colorado Outdoor & Ski Assn., PO Box 18598, Denver CO ; call: 303-470-9658.

January 21

Women's African Safari leaves for a tour featuring interactions with people as well as wildlife and sightseeing, through February 12. All women welcome, not limited to lesbians. Write: Womantrek, 1411 E. Olive Way, PO Box 20643, Seattle WA 98102; call: 206-325-4772.

January 26

Anniversary, Detroit Chapter of Black and White Men Together. For details, write: BWMT, 9354 East Outer Drive, Detroit MI 48213; phone: 313-525-9466.

Anniversary, Memphis Chapter of Black and White Men Together. For information, write: BWMT, 1471 North Parkway, Memphis TN 38122; phone: 901-726-1461.

Gay Men's Adventure Trip to New Zealand begins and continues through February 11, a "tramping trek" through five national parks. Write: Adventure Bound, 711 Walnut St., Carriage House, Boulder CO 80302; phone: 303-449-0990.

January 27

Overnight trip from San Francisco to Reno, Nev., sponsored by Girth and Mirth of Greater San Francisco, PO Box 528, San Francisco CA 94101. Events subject to change, so call the 24- Hour Hot Line: 415-552-1143.

January 31

Women's Dogsledding Trip in the northlands of Minnesota through February 4. Cost: $365. Write: Woodswomen, 25 W. Diamond Lake Rd., Minneapolis MN 55419; phone: 612-822-3809.

To Be Announced

Dance Marathon in New York City to benefit gay/lesbian senior citizens and seniors with AIDS, featuring seven decades of dance music, ballroom dancing, and live performances. Sponsored by Seniors Active in a Gay Environment (SAGE), 208 W. 13th St., New York City, NY 10011; call: 212-741-2247.

Board Meeting of Gay and Lesbian Parents Coalition International in Orlando, Fla. Write: GLPCI, Box 50360, Washington DC 20004; call: 703-548-3238 or 202-583-2158.

Ski weekend at Telluride and Monarch, write: Colorado Outdoor & Ski Assn., PO Box 18598, Denver CO ; call: 303-470-9658.

Sun	Mon	Tues	Wed	Thur	Fri	Sat
				1	2	3
4	5	6	7	8	9	10
11	12	13	14	15	16	17
18	19	20	21	22	23	24
25	26	27	28			

Gay/Lesbian Media Awareness Month
sponsored by the Gay and Lesbian Press Assn.
PO Box 8185, Universal City CA 91608-0185
818-880-4139

February 1

AIDS and Mental Health Educational Conference for professional care-givers begins in Anaheim, Calif., and continues through February 3, covering legal issues for mental health professionals working with HIV-infected and at-risk groups. Write: AIDS Health Project, 1855 Folsom St., Suite 506, San Francisco CA 94103; call: 415-476-6430.

Fifth Annual Rocky Mountain Regional Conference on AIDS runs through February 3 at the Radisson Hotel in Denver, attracting 600 to 800 medical and psychosocial professionals, teachers, and people with AIDS. Write: Colorado AIDS Project, 1576 Sherman St., Denver CO 80203; call: 303-837-0166.

February 2

Women's Cross-country Ski Weekend at Mt. Rainier in Washington State begins and continues through February 4. All women welcome, not limited to lesbians. Write: Womantrek, 1411 E. Olive Way, PO Box 20643, Seattle WA 98102; call: 206-325-4772.

February 3

Women's Tour of Thailand begins and continues through February 18, with stops in Bangkok and more remote areas in the north. All women welcome, not limited to lesbians. Write: Womantrek, 1411 E. Olive Way, PO Box 20643, Seattle WA 98102; call: 206-325-4772.

February 9

Russian River Square Dance Retreat through February 11 at Wildwood, Calif., sponsored by the Foggy City Dancers, PO Box 14324, San Francisco CA 94114; phone: 415-821-0417.

Bluegrass Classic Bowling Tournament in Louisville, Ky., begins and continues through February 11. Call: 502- 637-5361, or 458-5754.

Women's Cross-Country Ski Trip to Methow Valley in eastern Washington begins and continues through February 16, with slideshows, ice skating, and hot tub. All women welcome, not limited to lesbians. Write: Womantrek, 1411 E. Olive Way, PO Box 20643, Seattle WA 98102; call: 206-325-4772.

February 10

Sweetheart Valentine's Party in San Francisco, sponsored by Girth and Mirth of Greater San Francisco, PO Box 528, San Francisco CA 94101; Events subject to change, so call the 24- Hour Hot Line: 415-552-1143.

Women's Sea Kayaking Trip in the Gulf of California off Baja begins and continues through Feb. 17, with six days of paddling, snorkling, and wildlife-watching. All women welcome, not limited to lesbians. Write: Womantrek, 1411 E. Olive Way, PO Box 20643, Seattle WA 98102; call: 206-325-4772.

Women's Ski Weekend at White Pass in Washington State, for all levels, from beginners to experts, telemarkers, track skiers, downhill. Write: Woodswomen, 25 W. Diamond Lake Rd., Minneapolis MN 55419; phone: 612-822-3809.

February 12

Women's Trip to New Zealand with New Zealander guides begins and continues through February 26 (optional one-week extension). Write:

Woodswomen, 25 W. Diamond Lake Rd., Minneapolis MN 55419; phone: 612-822-3809.

February 13

Roll Aid Bowling Tournament in New York City. Call: 214-873-0154.

February 14

Third Annual Black Gay and Lesbian Leadership Conference begins at the Hyatt Regency Hotel in Atlanta, Ga., and continues through February 19. The first day's seminars are devoted to AIDS-related work--writing grant proposals, budgeting, program development, case management, and fund-raising techniques. Other events include strategy sessions for organizations, workshops on business, relationships, safer sex, and stress reduction, and an Awards Dinner Dance and Show. Write: BGLLF, PO Box 29812, Los Angeles CA 90027; call: 213-667-2549.

February 16

Dogsledding Trip for women begins in the North Country and continues through February 19, with luxurious living in a dome (beds, VCR, and microwave) plus snowshoeing and skiing. $250. Write: Women in the Wilderness, 566 Ottawa Ave., St. Paul MN 55107; call: 612-227.

Annual Convocation of the Unitarian-Universalists for Lesbian and Gay Concerns begins in Dallas and continues through February 19, with workshops, entertainment, and fellowship. Write the Unitarians at 25 Beacon St., Boston MA 02108; call: 207-283-3359.

Square Dance Fly-In "Flip Your Diamonds in Tinseltown" begins in Los Angeles and continues through February 18. Call: Tinseltown Squares at 213-937-7471.

Skiing Weekend at Mammoth Mountain sets out by deluxe chartered bus from Long Beach, Calif., for two nights at Meadowridge Condos. Write: The Gay and Lesbian Center of Long Beach, 2017 E. 4th St., Long Beach CA 90814; call: 213-434-4455.

G.A.G.M.E. 90 Bowling Tournament in Tampa, Fla., begins and continues through February 18. Call: 813-877-5627.

P.R.I.T. Bowling Tournament begins in Phoenix and continues through February 18.

A.C.E. Bowling Tournament in San Antonio continues through February 18. Call: 512-734-3630.

Rain Festival Square-Dance Fly-In in Seattle through February 18, hosted by the Puddletown Squares, PO Box 20671, Seattle WA 98102; call 206-324-8786.

February 17

Radical Women, an international organization of socialist feminists, holds its 23rd Anniversary Conference through February 20 in Los Angeles, with special emphasis on women of color, women workers, and lesbians. Write: Radical Feminists National Office, 523-A Valencia St., San Francisco CA 94110; call: 415-864-1278.

Women's Sea Kayaking Trip in the Gulf of California off Baja, through February 24. See Feb. 10 listing.

February 18

All-Gay "A Cruise to Remember" by RSVP Travel Productions sets sail from Miami for 7 days in the Caribbean aboard the SS *Sea Breeze,* with ports of call St. Barts, St. John, St. Thomas, and Puerto Plata. To book, call 303-467-7117 for the name of your local member of the International Gay Travel Assn. Or write: IGTA, PO Box 18247, Denver CO 80218.

Political Fundraising Dinner in Chicago, sponsored by IMPACT, Chicago's Gay and Lesbian Political Action Committee, at the Chicago Hilton Hotel and Towers. Cocktails begin at 5:30 p.m., in the Normandie Lounge, followed by dinner at 7:00 p.m., in the Grand Ballroom. Black tie optional. Write: IMPACT, 2835 N. Sheffield, Suite 209, Chicago IL 60657; call: 312-880-2308.

Women's Rafting Day Trip on Washington's Skagit River to view eagles and other wildlife. No rafting experience necessary for 10 mile stretch of calm water. All women welcome, not limited to lesbians. Write: Womantrek, 1411 E. Olive Way, PO Box 20643, Seattle WA 98102; call: 206-325-4772.

Third Indoor Gay Rodeo in Seattle, featuring square dancing and other Western activities. Entry fees for participation and $5.00 cover charge at the door. For more information, write Puddletown Squares, PO Box 20671, Seattle WA 98102.

February 24

Potluck with a Love Theme, for antique auto buffs in Oregon, sponsored by Northwest Scenic Cruisers, 206-254-1995.

February 25

Women's Winter Escape to Mexico begins and continues through March 6, featuring stops at beach resorts and Aztec ruins plus Mexico City. All women welcome, not limited to lesbians. Write: Womantrek, 1411 E. Olive Way, PO Box 20643, Seattle WA 98102; call: 206-325-4772.

February 27

Women's Tour of Costa Rica's magnificent rainforest begins and continues through March 9, featuring a stay at the Tiskita Biological Reserve to watch rare birds and sample exotic fruits. All women welcome, not limited to lesbians. Write: Womantrek, 1411 E. Olive Way, PO Box 20643, Seattle WA 98102; call: 206-325-4772.

Mardi Gras celebrated in New Orleans and other southern cities as well as Sydney, Australia, Rio and other Latin American spots.

February 28

Ash Wednesday Service at Reconciliation Metropolitan Community Church, 300 Graceland NE, Grand Rapids, Mich. Write: Reconciliation MCC, PO Box 1259; Grand Rapids MI 49501; call: 616-364-7633.

To Be Announced

Cross-Country Skifest for gays and lesbians at Lake Tahoe. For details, call 415-267-3027.

Valentine's Day Dance at Stanford University in California for men and women, with live D.J.; $3.00 admission. Sponsored by Lesbian, Gay, and Bisexual Community Center, PO Box 8265, Stanford CA 94309; call: 415-723-1488.

Ski Trip for gays and lesbians to Purgatory and Wolf Creek, sponsored by Colorado Outdoor & Ski Assn., PO Box 18598, Denver CO ; call: 303-470-9658.

Sunburst Dancer's Anniversary Celebration at Charlie's in Phoenix. Write: Sunburst Dancers. 9005 S. 19th Ave., Phoenix AZ 85041; phone: 602-268-5827.

Valentine's Dance in Kalamazoo, Mich., at the Peoples Church. For exact date, write: Lavender Morning, PO Box 729, Kalamazoo MI 49005, phone: 616-685-5377.

Concert in Santa Cruz, Calif., by the Santa Cruz Men's Chorus. For date, place, and time, call: 408-427-2722.

Valentine's Square Dance in New York City. Write: Times Squares, PO Box 1229 Ansonia Station, New York NY 10023.

Sun	Mon	Tues	Wed	Thur	Fri	Sat
				1	2	3
4	5	6	7	8	9	10
11	12	13	14	15	16	17
18	19	20	21	22	23	24
25	26	27	28	29	30	31

National Women's History Month

March 1

Dogsledding trip for women in the North Woods through March 4, with "old-homestead" accommodations and an expert dogsledding teacher. $325. Write: Women in the Wilderness, 566 Ottawa Ave., St. Paul MN 55107; call: 612-227-2284.

March 2

Midwest Regional Conference of Presbyterians for Lesbian and Gay Concerns meets in Minneapolis for support, worship, and fun through March 4. Write: Presbyterians for Lesbian and Gay Concerns, PO Box 38, New Brunswick NJ 08903-0038; call: 201-846-1510.

Women's Cross-Country Ski Weekend to Mt. Baker in Washington State continues through March 4. All women welcome, not limited to lesbians. Write: Womantrek, 1411 E. Olive Way, PO Box 20643, Seattle WA

98102; call: 206-325-4772.

Anniversary, Philadelphia Chapter of Black and White Men Together, through March 4. Write: 204 Haws Ave. Norristown PA 19491; phone: 215-277-8767.

March 3

Backpacking Trip for Women at Point of the Arches in Washington State. A great experience for women new to backpacking. Write: Woodswomen, 25 W. Diamond Lake Rd., Minneapolis MN 55419; phone: 612-822-3809.

March 4

All-Gay "A Cruise to Remember" by RSVP Travel Productions sets sail from Miami for 7 days in the Caribbean aboard the SS *Sea Breeze*, with ports of call St. Barts, St. John, St. Thomas, and Puerto Plata. To book, call 303-467-7117 for the name of your local member of the International Gay Travel Assn. Or write: IGTA, PO Box 18247, Denver CO 80218.

Benefit for the Gay/Lesbian Center in Long Beach, Calif., at the Terrace Theater for a Civic Light Opera special performance of "Follies," by Stephen Sondheim. Write: The Gay and Lesbian Center of Long Beach, 2017 E. 4th St., Long Beach CA 90814; call: 213-434-4455.

March 9

Spring Break Invitational Bowling Tournament in Ft. Lauderdale, Fla. Call: 305-462-0342.

March 10

All-Gay RSVP Cruise to Mexico's Yucatan Peninsula sails from New Orleans aboard the SS *Queen of Bermuda*, with stops at Key West, Playa del Carmen, and Cozumel. To book, call 303-467-7117 for the name of your local member of the International Gay Travel Assn. Or write: IGTA, PO Box 18247, Denver CO 80218.

Purim Carnival and Masked Ball in North Miami Beach, sponsored by Congregation Etz Chaim, 19094 W. Dixie Hwy., North Miami Beach FL 33180; call: 305-931-9318.

Women's Ski Trip to Sun Valley, Idaho begins and continues through March 17, with both downhill and cross-country opportunities. All women welcome, not limited to lesbians. Write: Womantrek, 1411 E. Olive Way, PO Box 20643, Seattle WA 98102; call: 206-325-4772.

March 11

Band concert in Chicago at 3:07 sharp! by the Great Lakes Freedom Band. For location, call: 312-935-6621.

March 12

AIDS Walk in Long Beach, 10 kilometers down the length of the beach to raise funds for persons with AIDS. Write: The Gay and Lesbian Center of Long Beach, 2017 E. 4th St., Long Beach CA 90814; call: 213-434-4455.

Women's Trek Through Sikkim, a small country on the Tibet border, begins and continues through April 3. Porters carry gear. Guide is Daku Tenzing Norgay, wife of the late Sherpa guide who led expedition to Mt. Everest summit. All women welcome, not limited to lesbians. Write: Womantrek, 1411 E. Olive Way, PO Box 20643, Seattle WA 98102; call: 206-325-4772.

March 13

Gay/Lesbian Gathering in Hawaii at the Kalani Honua Health & Beach Ranch for personal growth and adventure, through March 23. Repeated March 26 through April 1. Write: Kalani Honua, Inc. Box 4500, Pahoa-Kalapana, HI 96778. call: 808-965-7828.

Women's Tour of Costa Rica's magnificent rainforest begins and continues through March 23. All women welcome, not limited to lesbians. Write: Womantrek, 1411 E. Olive Way, PO Box 20643, Seattle WA 98102; call: 206-325-4772.

Women's Biking and Snorkeling Trip to Cozumel begins and continues through March 19 for $745. Write: Woodswomen, 25 W. Diamond Lake Rd., Minneapolis MN 55419; phone: 612-822-3809.

March 16

Annual convention of the Association for Gay, Lesbian, and Bisexual Issues in Counseling begins and continues through March 19 in Cincinnati, Ohio. Write them at Box 216, Jenkintown PA 19046.

English Bay Cup Bowling Tournament in Vancouver, Canada. Call: 604-685-1858.

March 17

St. Patrick's Day Dinner Dance, a fundraiser for Dignity Metro New Jersey at St. George's Church in Maplewood, N.J. Write c/o Box M, St. George's Church, 550 Ridgewood Ave., Maplewood NJ 07040.

Joint Concert in Boston at Symphony Hall with the Seattle Men's Chorus and the Boston Gay Men's Chorus. Write: Boston Gay Men's Chorus, PO Box 1348, Back Bay Annex, Boston MA 02117; call: 617-482-2527.

Eighth Anniversary of the Western Star Dancers in San Francisco, with a national caller. Write: Western Star Dancers, 584 Castro St. Suite 480, San Francisco CA 94114; call: 415-864-6134 or 415-621-0862.

Tour of Freightliner Truck Mfg. for Oregon auto enthusiasts, sponsored by Northwest Scenic Cruisers, 206-254-1995.

March 20

SCUBA Diving for Women at the Yucatan's Palancar Reef off Cozumel begins and continues through March 26. Write: Woodswomen, 25 W. Diamond Lake Rd., Minneapolis MN 55419; phone: 612-822-3809.

March 22

Fifteenth Annual Southeast Conference for Lesbians and Gay Men begins at the Radisson Plaza Hotel in Raleigh N.C., and continues through March 25. The theme is "Working to Strengthen Our Southeastern Communities," and there will be more than 60 workshops, major speakers, and entertainment.

March 23

Skiing Weekend at Mammoth Mountain, leaves from Long Beach on a chartered bus for two nights at Meadowridge Condos. Write: The Gay and Lesbian Center of Long Beach, 2017 E. 4th St., Long Beach CA 90814; call: 213-434-4455.

March 24

All-Gay Mexican Riviera Cruise by RSVP Travel Productions begins at San Diego and continues aboard the SS *Bermuda Star* through March 31, with ports of call that include Puerto Vallarta, Mazatlan, and Cabo San Lucas. To book, call 303-467-7117 for the name of your local member of the International Gay Travel Assn. Or write: IGTA, PO Box 18247, Denver CO 80218.

Annual St. Patrick's Day/Easter Season Party in San Francisco, sponsored by Girth and Mirth of Greater San Francisco, PO Box 528, San Francisco CA 94101; Events subject to change, so call the 24- Hour Hot Line: 415-552-1143.

Concert in Chicago by the Windy City Gay Chorus, 8:07 p.m. sharp! at the Preston Bradley Center. For ticket information, call: 312-404-9242.

March 26

Mr. Gay Columbus Contest, with service to the gay/lesbian community one of the criteria along with personal beauty. Write: Stonewall Union, PO Box 10814, Columbus, OH 43201-7814; call: 614-299-7764.

March 28

Dinah Shore Golf Tournament begins in Palm Springs, Calif., and continues through April 1, attracting hundreds of lesbians to this posh desert resort area. There are several huge lesbian parties and dances at the major hotels, and every gay resort in the region becomes a lesbian resort for the weekend. Reservations far in advance are a must. For help in booking, contact your local International Gay Travel Association Agent.

March 29

Lavender Images IV--A Lesbian and Gay Film Series in Minneapolis begins and continues through May 31 at the University of Minnesota, Willey Hall 125, on the West Bank Campus, featuring ten evenings of lesbian and gay feature films. Write: Coffman Union Film Program, 220 Coffman Union, 300 Washington Ave. SE, University of Minnesota, Minneapolis MN 55455, call: 612-625-8685.

March 30

Spring Concert by the Gay Men's Chorus of Washington, D.C., at the Lisner Auditorium, featuring popular music of the late 1950s and early 1960s. Write: Gay Men's Chorus of Washington, PO Box 57043, Washington DC 20037; call: 202-338-SING.

T.R.E.A.T. Bowling Tournament in Pittsburgh, Pa., call: 412-922-4711, 321-3251.

Golden State Gay Rodeo begins in Los Angeles and continues through April 1, with horse events, wild-bull riding, calf roping, and steer decorating. For details, write Golden State Gay Rodeo, PO Box 691865, Los Angeles, CA 90069. Call: 213-498-1675.

March 31

Dinner/Dance in Chicago to benefit Horizons Community Services for gay men and lesbians, with a silent action and awards presentations; black-tie optional. Write: Horizons, 3225 N. Sheffield Ave., Chicago 60657; call: 312-472-6469.

Women's Trek Through Central Nepal begins and continues through April 23, with porters to carry gear. All women welcome, not limited to lesbians. Write: Womantrek, 1411 E. Olive Way, PO Box 20643, Seattle WA 98102; call: 206-325-4772.

To Be Announced

Annual Conference of Lesbian, Gay, and Bisexual People in Medicine in Washington DC. For exact dates and details, write them c/o American Medical Student Assn., 1890 Preston White Dr., Reston VA 22091;

call: 703-620-6600.

Tri-City Invitational Bowling Tournament in San Jose, Calif.

Everglades Canoe Trip for women. No experience needed for this easy-going outing with great food and experienced guides. Women of all ages welcome. Write: Women in the Wilderness, 566 Ottawa Ave., St. Paul MN 55107; call: 612-227

Board Meeting of Gay and Lesbian Parents Coalition International in Dallas, Tex. Write: GLPCI, Box 50360, Washington DC 20004; call: 703-548-3238 or 202-583-2158.

Ski Weeks for gay and lesbians in Steamboat Springs, Taos, and Alta/ Snowbird, organized by: Colorado Outdoor & Ski Assn., PO Box 18598, Denver CO ; call: 303-470-9658.

Square dance Fly-in in the Miami-Ft. Lauderdale area, sponsored by the South Florida Mustangs, PO Box 462, Hollywood FL 33022; call: 305-925-7435.

Eighth Anniversary of Raffles Bar and Restaurant in Philadelphia, 243 S. Camac St., Philadelphia PA 19107, 215-545-6969.

Women's History Month Activities in West Hollywood, Calif., include music, theater, workshops, forums, and the conclusion of an exhibition of the work of 20 women artists at the West Hollywood City Hall. For a calendar of events, write: City of West Hollywood, 8611 Santa Monica Blvd., West Hollywood, CA 90069.

Annual Dinner of the Bar Association for Human Rights of Greater New York is to be held in New York City, with prominent speakers and presentation of awards to outstanding supporters of gay/lesbian rights. Write them at PO Box 1899, Grand Central Sta., New York NY 10163.

Are Your Organization's Activities Listed Here?

If not, they should be. Don't miss out next year. Send your 1991 events to:

ENVOY ENTERPRISES
740 N. Rush St., Suite 609
Chicago IL 60611

Sun	Mon	Tues	Wed	Thur	Fri	Sat
1	2	3	4	5	6	7
8	9	10	11	12	13	14
15	16	17	18	19	20	21
22	23	24	25	26	27	28
29	30					

April 1

Women's Rock Climbing Expedition to Joshua Tree Monument in California. Beginners learn the basics of getting off the ground and staying on the rocks. There is also a program for intermediates. Trip runs through April 7. Write: Woodswomen, 25 W. Diamond Lake Rd., Minneapolis MN 55419; phone: 612-822-3809.

April 6

Annual Northwest Swapmeet for antique auto buffs in Oregon, through April 8. Call Northwest Scenic Cruisers, 206-254-1995.

April 7

Annual Dinner of the Bay Area Municipal Elections Committee (BAYMEC) at the Fairmont Hotel in San Jose, Calif., billed as the largest gay and lesbian political event in the South Bay Area. Tickets are $100 per person. Write: BAYMEC, PO Box 90070, San Jose CA 95109; call: 408-297-1024.

Pre-Convention Square Dance in Portland, sponsored by the Rosetown Ramblers, PO Box 5352, Portland OR 97228; call: 503-274-4271.

Concert in Des Moines, Iowa, by the Des Moines Men's Chorus, at the Iowa State Historical Building, 600 E. Locust St. For more details, write the chorus at 1534 47th St., Des Moines IA 50311; call: 515-255-1684.

Concert in Pasadena, Calif., by the Gay Men's Chorus of Los Angeles, at Pasadena Presbyterian Church, 54 N. Oakland Ave. For ticket information, write the chorus at 7985 Santa Monica Blvd. #109-134, West Hollywood, CA 90046; phone: 213-462-5284.

April 8

Concert in West Los Angeles by the Gay Men's Chorus of Los Angeles at 4:00 p.m. For location, write or call at the above (April 7) address.

Concert in Denver by the Denver Gay Men's Chorus "Prom Night 1949" at Mammoth Events Center, 8:00 p.m. Write: Denver Gay Men's Chorus, PO Box 6717, Denver CO 80202; phone: 303-331-2302.

April 10

Passover. Many gay/lesbian Jewish groups hold seders. For a list of Jewish organizations, see page 96

Pre-Convention Square Dance in Seattle, hosted by the Puddletown Squares, PO Box 20671, Seattle WA 98102, 206-324-8786.

Passover Seder (second night) in North Miami Beach. Congregation Etz Chaim, 19094 W. Dixie Hwy., North Miami Beach FL 33180; call: 305-931-9318.

April 12

North Star Promenade, the annual convention of the International Association of Gay Square Dance Clubs begins at the Hotel Vancouver in Vancouver, B.C., and continues through April 15. Hosted by Squares Across the Border, PO Box 4404 Main Post Office, Vancouver, B.C., CANADA V6B 3Z8. Call: 604-683-6008. Convention contact: North Star Promenade, PO Box 2731, Vancouver, B.C., Canada, V6B 3X2; phone: 604-873-9303.

Maunday Thursday Service at Reconciliation Metropolitan Community Church, 300 Graceland NE, Grand Rapids, Mich. Write: Reconciliation MCC, PO Box 1259; Gand Rapids MI 49501; call: 616-364-7633.

APOLLO Bowling Tournament in Calgary, Canada, begins and continues through April 15. Call: 403-244-8045.

April 13

Good Friday Service at Reconciliation MCC in Grand Rapids, Mich. See April 12.

American Gay Atheists Annual Meeting begins and continues through April 15 in Tampa/St. Petersburg, Fla. Lectures, workshops, dinners, and entertainment, held in conjuction with the 1990 American Atheist Convention. Write: American Gay Atheists, PO Box 66711, Houston TX 77266-6711; call: 713-880-4242.

Dixie Invitational X Bowling Tournament in Atlanta, Ga. Call: 404-938-8716 or 451-3291.

M.A.K.I.T. Bowling Tournament in Kansas City. Call: 816-931-9608.

April 14

Concert in Portland, Ore., by the Portland Gay Men's Chorus, featuring a female jazz vocalist, 8:00 p.m. at Arlene Schnitzer Concert Hall. Write the chorus at PO Box 3223, Portland, OR 97208, or call: 503-227-7907.

April 15

Easter Sunday. All Metropolitan Community Churches hold Easter services. To find the church nearest you, see page 93.

Sunrise Service and Easter Worship Service at Reconciliation Metropolitan Community Church, 300 Graceland NE, Grand Rapids, Mich. Write: Reconciliation MCC, PO Box 1259; Gand Rapids MI 49501; call: 616-364-7633.

Easter Sunrise Service in Huntsville, Ala. Write: Metropolitan Community Church of Huntsville, PO Box 10021, Huntsville AL 35801; call: 205-533-6220.

April 18

Merrie Monarch Hula Festival in Hawaii at the Kalani Honua Health & Beach Ranch provides immersion for gays and lesbians in Hawaiian culture, language, and history. Attend the Big Island's nightly hula dance competition; side-trip to spectacular Volcanoes National Park. Write: Kalani Honua, Inc. Box 4500, Pahoa-Kalapana, HI 96778; call: 808-965-7828.

April 20

Funlovers Bowling Tournament in Garden Gove, Calif., begins and continues through April 22. Call: 714-826-0927.

Women's Trek to Mt. Everest Base Camp in Nepal begins and continues through May 11. Cost: $1,995. Write: Woodswomen, 25 W. Diamond Lake Rd., Minneapolis MN 55419; phone: 612-822-3809.

April 21

Women's Sea Kayaking Trip in the Gulf of California off Baja begins and continues through April 29, with six days of paddling, snorkling, and wildlife-watching. All women welcome, not limited to lesbians. Write: Womantrek, 1411 E. Olive Way, PO Box 20643, Seattle WA 98102; call: 206-325-4772.

Spring Meeting of Affirmation/United Methodists begins in Kansas City, Mo., and continues through April 22. Write them at PO Box 1021, Evanston IL 60204; phone: 312-475-0499.

G.R.E.A.T. Bowling Tournament in Rochester, NY. Call 716-473-9948.

MIL-MA-IDS V Bowling Tournament in Madison, Wisc. Call: 608-273-9723.

Gay/Lesbian Gathering in Hawaii at the Kalani Honua Ranch, through April 29, featuring personal growth and adventure. See April 18 listing for address.

Women's Caribbean Trip to Puerto Rico and New Dawn's Retreat on the island of Vieques, begins and continues for eight unstructured days through April 28. Lodging in a dorm or tent. All women welcome, not limited to lesbians. Write: Womantrek, 1411 E. Olive Way, PO Box 20643, Seattle WA 98102; call: 206-325-4772.

April 22

Beginning Women's Rock Climbing Day in Washington State. Write: Woodswomen, 25 W. Diamond Lake Rd., Minneapolis MN 55419; phone: 612-822-3809.

April 25

Doubles Tennis Tournament at the Seattle Tennis Center to benefit IN TOUCH, a service agency that provides massage therapy for People with AIDS. Write: IN TOUCH, 600 E. Pine St., Seattle WA 98122; call: 206-684-4764.

April 28

Third European Conference of Gay and Lesbian Jews continues through May 1 in Amsterdam, The Netherlands, with special celebrations on April 30 centering around Israel Independence Day and Queens Day, a Dutch national holiday. Write: World Congress of Gay and Lesbian Jewish Organizations, PO Box 18961, Washington DC 20036.

Concert in Denver at the Corkin Theater by the Denver Women's Chorus. Write: 2686 4th St. Boulder Co 80304; call: 303-477-8702.

Women's Caribbean Trip to Puerto Rico and New Dawn's Retreat on the island of Vieques, through May 5. See April 21 listing.

Beginning Women's Rock Climbing Weekend in Washington State through April 29. Write: Woodswomen, 25 W. Diamond Lake Rd., Minneapolis MN 55419; phone: 612-822-3809.

United '90, Annual Conference in New Jersey of the Gay Activist Alliance of Morris County. An all-day conference with well-known speakers and about 30 workshops. Write: Gay Activist Alliance of Morris County, PO Box 137, Convent Station, NJ 07961-0137; phone: 201-282-1595.

April 30

Women's Bicycle Tour of China, through the spectacular Guilin karst formations along the Li River in the south, begins and continues through May 23. All women welcome, not limited to lesbians. Write: Womantrek, 1411 E. Olive Way, PO Box 20643, Seattle WA 98102; call: 206-325-4772.

Hiking Trip for Women in Utah's Desert Slickrock Country begins and continues through May 5. Write: Woodswomen, 25 W. Diamond Lake Rd., Minneapolis MN 55419; phone: 612-822-3809.

To Be Announced

Art Show and sale of works by local artists to benefit the Fourstates Community AIDS Project. Write: FSCAP, PO Box 3476, Joplin MO 64803-3476; call: 417-624-1250.

Ski Trip, BBQ, and Party at Loveland, Colo. For details, write: Colorado Outdoor & Ski Assn., PO Box 18598, Denver CO ; call: 303-470-9658.

All gay/lesbian tour of Hearst Castle, Morro Bay, and the Danish town of Solvang. Charter tour leaves from Long Beach. Write: The Gay and Lesbian Center of Long Beach, 2017 E. 4th St., Long Beach CA 90814; call: 213-434-4455.

Dancing and Camping Retreat for square dancers at Fife's Resort in California's Russian River area. For exact date, write: Capital City Squares, PO Box 19986, Sacramento CA 95819; call: 916-969-5153.

Benefit Theater Performance in San Francisco, for Shanti and other organizations, of "Ward 22, The Musical." Write: In-Sanity Productions, 584 Castro St. #643, San Francisco CA 94114-2588.

Concert in Minneapolis by the Calliope Women's Chorus. For date, place, and time, write them at 3353 31st Ave. S., Minneapolis MN 55406; or call: 612-377-1611.

Concert in Philadelphia by the Philadelphia Gay Men's Chorus. Write: PO Box 58842; phone: 215-732-5079.

Seventh Annual Bartender's Ball at Raffles in Philadelphia, 242 S. Camac St., 215-545-6969.

AIDS Cycle Challenge in West Hollywood is the largest AIDS-related cycling event in Southern California. Riders participate for pledged funds, all proceeds are donated to AIDS organizations. Event begins and ends across from the Pacific Design Center. Write: City of West Hollywood, 8611 Santa Monica Blvd., West Hollywood CA 90069.

Sun	Mon	Tues	Wed	Thur	Fri	Sat
		1	2	3	4	5
6	7	8	9	10	11	12
13	14	15	16	17	18	19
20	21	22	23	24	25	26
27	28	29	30	31		

Gay and Lesbian Travel Month

sponsored by the International Gay Travel Association, to promote awareness of gay/lesbian owned and operated resorts and tour companies and the many local gay/lesbian travel agents available to serve the special needs of our community. Write: IGTA, PO Box 18247, Denver CO 80218, or call:303-467-7117.

May 1

Gay and Lesbian Awareness Week at Stanford University, the first week in May, a series of concerts, lectures, dances, and other activities to reach out and educate the general Stanford community. Sponsored by Lesbian, Gay, and Bisexual Community Center, PO Box 8265, Stanford CA 94309; call: 415-723-1488.

May 4

Gay and Lesbian Press Association's 10th Annual International Convention begins and continues through May 7 in San Francisco, featuring workshops, seminars, guest speakers, networking opportunities, social events, and the presentation of the annual press awards. Write GALPA, PO Box 8185, Universal City CA 91608-0185; call: 818-902-1476.

Gotham Open Bowling Tournament begins in New York City and continues through May 6. Call: 718-784-0903; 212-246-5912.

Anniversary, Baltimore Chapter, Black and White men Together, through May 6. Write: BWMT, 3710 Lochraven, Baltimore MD 21218; phone: 301-235-5338.

May 5

Intermediate Women's Rock Climbing Weekend in Washington State through May 6. Write: Woodswomen, 25 W. Diamond Lake Rd., Minneapolis MN 55419; phone: 612-822-3809.

May 12

Sixth Annual Bike-A-Thon in San Francisco, a fund-raising bicycle event to raise money for organizations providing direct services to persons with AIDS. Sponsored by Different Spokes, PO Box 14711, San Francisco CA 94114-0711; phone: 415-282-1647.

"Sweet Sixteen", the Sixteenth Anniversary Dinner Dance of Congregation Etz Chaim, 19094 W. Dixie Hwy., North Miami Beach FL 33180; call: 305-931-9318.

Women's Mountaineering Trip in Washington's Cascade Mountain Range begins and continues through May 13. Write: Woodswomen, 25 W. Diamond Lake Rd., Minneapolis MN 55419; phone: 612-822-3809.

May 15

Road Rally in Oregon for Antique Car Buffs. For details, contact the Northwest Scenic Cruisers at 206-254-1995.

May 16

Annual Convention of the International Gay Travel Association begins in Key West, Fla., and continues through May 20. Write: IGTA, PO Box 18247, Denver CO 80218, or call:303-467-7117.

May 18

Womongathering: The Festival of Womyn's Spirituality begins and continues through May 20 near Oxford, Pa., featuring experiential workshops conducted by nationally known spiritual leaders. Write: Campfest Festivals, RR 5, Box 185, Franklinville NJ 08322; call: 609-694-2037.

Square Dance Fly-In at Rehoboth Beach, Del., gathers at the Atlantic Budget Inn, through May 20, sponsored by Chesapeake Squares, 509 E. 35th St., Baltimore MD 21218; call: 301-366-7074.

May 19

Long Beach (Calif.) Gay Pride Parade and Festival begins and continues through May 20 with dancing, entertainment, food, information booths, and the parade. Write: The Gay and Lesbian Center of Long Beach, 2017 E. 4th St., Long Beach CA 90814; call: 213-434-4455.

May 20

Seventh Annual Worldwide AIDS Candlelight Memorial. Vigils and candlelight memorials are held around the world in more than 30 countries and 200 cities, making this the world's largest single AIDS action. The events are sponsored by local AIDS organizations to honor the men, women, and children who have died of AIDS and to provide public support of those now fighting the disease. The international organizer of the memorial is: Mobilization Against AIDS. 1540 Market St., Suite 60, San Francisco CA 94102; phone: 415-863-4676.

Trip to Alaska's Ruth Glacier for Women begins and continues through May 26. Cost: $645. Write: Woodswomen, 25 W. Diamond Lake Rd., Minneapolis MN 55419; phone: 612-822-3809.

May 24

CAMPFEST: The Comfortable Womyn's Music Festival begins and continues through May 28 near Oxford, Pa., with music, tennis, swimming in Olympic-size pool, and accommodations in dorm-style cabins or tents. Vegetarian and non-vegetarian meals provided. Write: Campfest Festivals, RR 5, Box 185, Franklinville NJ 08322; call: 609-694-2037.

IGBO X, the International Gay/Lesbian Bowling Tournament begins in Los Angeles and continues through May 28, with bowlers from all over the United States and Canada. Call: 213-539-4926.

Southern Women's Music & Comedy Festival begins and continues through May 28 at a private campground in Georgia, about 80 miles northeast of Atlanta. Many stages with music and comedy; workshops, swimming, dances, crafts. Camping, cabin, and R.V. tickets. Write: Robin Tyler Productions, 15842 Chase St., Sepulveda CA 91343; Phone: 818-893-4075.

May 25

Eighth Anniversary Celebration of Black and White Men Together of Memphis, Tenn., begins and continues through May 28 with barbecue and other social events surrounding the Memphis in May International Festival. Write BWMT Memphis, PO Box 412773, Memphis TN 38174; call: 901-726-1461.

Spring Round-Up at Agape Acres through May 28 in East Jordan, Mich., sponsored by Reconciliation Metropolitan Community Church, PO Box 1259; Grand Rapids MI 49501; call: 616-364-7633.

Milwaukee Classic Softball Tournament begins at Mitchell Domes Park and continues through May 27, with three divisions: Competitive, Recreation, and Women. Awards banquet and parties. Write: Saturday Softball League, PO Box 92605, Milwaukee WI 53202.

Oklahoma Gay Rodeo begins and continues through the Memorial Day Weekend, with horse events, wild-bull riding, calf roping, and steer decorating. Write: OGRA, PO Box 12485, Oklahoma City OK 73157.

May 25

International Mr. Leather Contest begins in Chicago and continues through the Memorial Day Weekend with four days and nights of parties. International Mr. Leather will be chosen Sunday night, May 27. Write: International Mr. Leather, Inc., 5025 N. Clark St., Chicago IL 60640: phone: 312-878-6360.

May 26

Reception for Lesbian Alumnae of Mount Holyoke College, at the college, sponsored by the Mount Holyoke College Lesbian Alumnae Network. All bisexual and lesbian alumnae attending the reunion of classes are welcome. A closed party for network members only follows. Write: Mount Holyoke College Network, 119 Dakota St., Dorchester MA 02124; or call: 617-265-0124.

United States Gay Open Tennis Tournament begins in the San Francisco Bay Area and continues through Memorial Day Weekend. Men and women, open B, C, and over 35 divisions, singles and doubles will be played at the University of California at Berkeley and City College of San Francisco. Write: Gay Tennis Federation of San Francisco, 2215-R Market St., Suite 109, San Francisco CA 94115; call: 415-563-8568.

Dance at Nomad Village, Bethany Beach, Del., to benefit the Gay and Lesbian Alliance of Delaware. $3.00 at the door, gifts for the first 100 people. Write: GLAD, 214 Market St., Wilmington DE 19801; call: 302-655-5280.

May 27

Annual General Assembly of Presbyterians for Lesbian and Gay Concerns meets in Salt Lake City for eight days of worship and witnessing to the Presbyterian Church (USA). Events include a hospitality suite and an exhibition booth. Write: Presbyterians for Lesbian and Gay Concerns, PO Box 38, New Brunswick NJ 08903-0038; call: 201-846-1510.

Gay Windjammer Cruise aboard the *Yankee Clipper* departs from Antigua for six nights in the Caribbean. To book, call 303-467-7117 for the name of your local member of the International Gay Travel Assn. Or write: IGTA, PO Box 18247, Denver CO 80218.

Annual meeting of the Assn. of Gay and Lesbian Psychiatrists in New York City, in conjunction with the American Psychiatric Assn. convention. Write: 1732 S.E. Ash, Portland OR 97214.

To Be Announced

Ski Trip and Luau at Arapahoe Basin for gays and lesbians plus a Hot Springs Weekend. Write: Colorado Outdoor & Ski Assn., PO Box 18598, Denver CO ; call: 303-470-9658.

Grand Canyon (Arizona) Charter Tour for two nights for gays and lesbians. Write: The Gay and Lesbian Center of Long Beach, 2017 E. 4th St., Long Beach CA 90814; call: 213-434-4455.

Women's Walking Tour of Scotland has been tentatively planned. For confirmation and information, write: Womantrek, 1411 E. Olive Way, PO Box 20643, Seattle WA 98102; call: 206-325-4772.

BEWARE!

Even the best planned events are subject to change. Before making travel arrangements or otherwise obligating yourself to attend a function listed, please call or write the sponsoring group to be sure the date or place has not been changed.

Sun	Mon	Tues	Wed	Thur	Fri	Sat
					1	2
3	4	5	6	7	8	9
10	11	12	13	14	15	16
17	18	19	20	21	22	23
24	25	26	27	28	29	30

National Lobby Days

to create grass-roots pressure at the congressional district level for laws supporting gay/lesbian rights, conducted by the National Gay & Lesbian Task Force, 1517 U St. NW, Washington, D.C. 20009

June 1

Second Annual Awards Reception sponsored by the AIDS Center of Queens County, N.J., at the New York Hall of Science in Flushing Meadows, NY. Write: ACQC, 97-45 Queens Blvd., Suite 1220, Rego Park NY 11374; call: 718-896-2500.

June 2

Gay and Lesbian Parents Coalition International holds its annual conference in Washington, D.C., through June 3. Write: GLPCI, Box 50360, Washington DC 20004; call: 703-548-3238 or 202-583-2158.

Affiliated Big Men's Clubs West Coast Conference. For exact location, write: Girth and Mirth of Greater San Francisco, PO Box 528, San Francisco CA 94101; or call the 24- Hour Hot Line: 415-552-1143.

Rosebowl Classic VI Bowling Tournament in Portland, Ore., continues through June 3. Call: 503-293-0438.

People's Fair in Denver's gay Capitol Hill neighborhood, including booths and activities by/for gays and lesbians. This date is tentative, and the event may be scheduled for the weekend of June 9 & 10. Check it out with Colorado Gay and Lesbian Task Force, PO Box 18632, Denver CO 80218; call: 303-830-2981.

Women's Mountaineering Trip to the Cascade Range of Washington State begins and continues through June 3. Write: Woodswomen, 25 W. Diamond Lake Rd., Minneapolis MN 55419; phone: 612-822-3809.

Whitewater Raft Trip in Oregon, sponsored by the Northwest Scenic Cruisers antique auto club. Call: 206-254-1995.

June 3

Philadelphia's Gay and Lesbian Pride Parade and Festival in the downtown Center City area. Write: Parade '90, 1312 Spruce St. #3-B, Philadelphia PA 19107; call: 215-545-2836.

June 8

Gay/Lesbian trip to Yosemite National Park departs from Long Beach for two nights at Curry Village private cabins and a tour of the park, hiking, and beautiful day and night vistas on this full-moon weekend. Write: The Gay and Lesbian Center of Long Beach, 2017 E. 4th St., Long Beach CA 90814; call: 213-434-4455.

G.I.F.T. Bowling Tournament in Cleveland, Ohio begins and continues through June 10. Call: 216-228-3875.

Women's Leadership Development Experience, centering around a canoe trip through Minnesota's Boundary Waters, begins and continues through June 17. Write: Woodswomen, 25 W. Diamond Lake Rd., Minneapolis MN 55419; phone: 612-822-3809.

June 9

Concert in Long Beach, Calif., by the Gay Men's Chorus of Long Beach, at the Ebell Theater, 3rd and Cerrito. Write them at 2017 E. 4th St., Long Beach CA 90814; or phone: 213-434-6093.

Beginning Women's Rock Climbing Weekend in Washington State through June 10. Write: Woodswomen, 25 W. Diamond Lake Rd., Minneapolis MN 55419; phone: 612-822-3809.

June 10

Band Concert in Chicago at 3:07 sharp! by the Great Lakes Freedom Band. For location, call: 312-935-6621.

June 15

International Lesbian and Gay Film Festival in San Francisco begins and continues through June 24. For more information, write: Frameline, PO Box 14792, San Francisco CA 94114; call: 415-861-5245.

Louisiana State Gay and Lesbian Conference, Celebration '90, begins at the Hyatt Regency in New Orleans and continues through June 17. Write: Celebration '90, PO Box 51877, New Orleans LA 70151; call: 504-586-8638.

Student Awareness Week, sponsored by the Gay Youth Coalition, in the San Francisco Bay Area through June 24. A series of events and activities focus on gay youth and student issues. Write: GYCC, PO Box 846, San Francisco CA 94101-0846; or call the Gay Area Youth Switchboard: 415-386-GAYS.

Pride Concert in Boston at Jordan Hall, New England Conservatory. For ticket information, write: Boston Gay Men's Chorus, PO Box 1348, Back Bay Annex, Boston MA 02117; call: 617-482-2527.

June 16

Gay/Lesbian Pride Week in Columbus, Ohio, begins and continues through June 24, with events that include a Gay/Lesbian Film Festival, poetry readings, lectures, religious services, art show, social events, and candlelight vigil, ending with a march and rally and GayFest II. Write: Stonewall Union, PO Box 10814, Columbus OH 43201-7814; call: 614-299-7764.

Pride Parade in Milwaukee, Wisc., kicks off lesbian/gay pride week, which includes concerts, lectures. educational activities, and parties. Write: ML/GPC. 225 South 2nd St., Milwaukee WI 53204., or call: 414-32-PRIDE.

Pride Concert by the Gay Men's Chorus of Washington, D.C., in the Lisner Auditorium, featuring music by gay composers. Write: Gay Men's Chorus of Washington, PO Box 57043, Washington DC 20037; call: 202-338-SING.

Pride Concert in Boston. (See June 15.)

GayFest begins in Columbus, Ohio, featuring a gay/lesbian film festival, religious services, lectures, concerts, softball, theater and poetry readings, workshops, and ends with a Pride Parade and Rally on June 24. Write: Stonewall Union, PO Box 10814, Columbus OH 10814; call: 614-299-7764.

Annual Business Meeting of Unitarian Universalists for Lesbian and Gay Concerns. For location, write 25 Beacon St., Boston MA 02108, or call: 617-742-2100.

Pride Concert in Chicago by the Windy City Gay Chorus at Orchestra Hall, 8:07 sharp! Call: 312-404-9242.

Intermediate Women's Rock Climbing Weekend in Washington State through June 17. Write: Woodswomen, 25 W. Diamond Lake Rd., Minneapolis MN 55419; phone: 612-822-3809.

June 17

Gay Pride Ecumenical Service and Celebration in Grand Rapids, Mich., at Reconciliation Metropolitan Community Church, 300 Graceland NE, Grand Rapids, Mich. Write: Reconciliation MCC, PO Box 1259; Grand Rapids MI 49501; call: 616-364-7633.

Women's Rafting Trip on Oregon's Deschutes River begins and continues through June 22, with fishing, swimming, hiking, and whitewater. All women welcome, not limited to lesbians. Write: Womantrek, 1411 E. Olive Way, PO Box 20643, Seattle WA 98102; call: 206-325-4772.

June 20

Women's Trek through Peru begins and continues through July 10, to Cusco and Machu Picchu. All women welcome, not limited to lesbians. Write: Womantrek, 1411 E. Olive Way, PO Box 20643, Seattle WA 98102; call: 206-325-4772.

Sixth International Conference on AIDS, sponsored by the University of California, begins in San Francisco and continues through June 24, with the theme of "AIDS in the Nineties: From Science to Public Policy." For more information, write: Sixth Annual Conference on AIDS, UCSF, Box 1505, San Francisco CA 94143-1505, phone: 415-550-0880, fax: 415-550-0886.

June 21

International Bisexual Conference in San Francisco through June 24. For details, sponsored by BiPOL, the Bay Area bisexual/gay/lesbian political organization and the North American Bisexual Network. Contact: BiPOL, 584 Castro St. #422, San Francisco CA 94114; phone: 415-759-NABN.

June 22

Chicago Pride-Week Invitational bowling tournament begins and continues through June 24. Call: 312-769-5115, 769-5869, or 865-5706.

Golden Threads annual celebration of older lesbians, in Provincetown, Mass., through June 24. Write c/o PO Box 3177, Burlington VT 05401.

June 23

Physique '90: National Lesbian and Gay Bodybuilding Championships are held at the Palace of Fine Arts in San Francisco. Write: Arcadia Body Building Society, Inc., 1455A Market St., Suite 221, San Francisco CA 94103; call: 415-431-6254.

Rocky Mountain Regional Lesbian & Gay Pride Parade. Could be scheduled for June 30-July 1. Write: Colorado Gay and Lesbian Task Force, PO Box 18632, Denver CO 80218; call: 303-830-2981.

New Orleans Gay Pride Parade and Festival through June 24 . Write: New Orleans Gay Pride, Inc., PO Box 72055, New Orleans LA 70172. call: 504-566-0329.

Pre-Pride Parade Square Dance in San Francisco. Write: Western Star Dancers, 584 Castro St., Suite 480, San Francisco CA 94114; call: 415-864-6134 or 415-621-0862.

Tenth Anniversary Concert of the Portland Gay Men's Chorus, at the Portland Center for the Performing Arts, 8:00 p.m. Write the chorus at PO Box 3223, Portland OR 97208; call: 503-227-7907.

Concert in Des Moines, Iowa, by the Des Moines Men's Chorus, at the Grand View College Auditorium. Write: 1534 47th St., Des Moines, IA 50311, or call: 515-255-1684,

Pride Concert in Denver with the Denver Gay Men's Chorus, Denver Women's Chorus, and the Twin Cities Men's Chorus. Write: Denver Gay Men's Chorus, PO Box 6717, Denver CO 80202; phone: 303-331-2302.

Annual Meeting of the Gay and Lesbian Task Force of the American Library Association begins in Chicago and continues through June 28 in conjunction with the annual ALA meeting. Write: American Library Assn., 50 E. Huron, Chicago IL 60611.

Gay Pride March in Columbia, South Carolina, (first ever!) to the State Capitol. Call the Palmetto Gay/Lesbian Alliance: 803-271-4207.

Gay Pride Festival in Brooklyn's Prospect Park Picnic House. Write: Gay Friends & Neighbors, 44 5th Ave., #147, Brooklyn NY 11217.

June 24

Concert in Portland at 7:00 p.m. See June 23 listing.

National Assn. of Black and White Men Together holds its annual conference, "Family--The Seed Grows," at Seven Hills Center, San Francisco State University through July 1. This event will feature workshops on racism, interracial relationships, partnership building, the media and gay people of color, plus dances, parties, a boat cruise, and picnic. For more information, write: NABWMT, 584 Castro St., Suite 140, San Francisco CA 94114; call: 415-431-1976, 415-826-4618, or 901-452-5894.

San Francisco's Lesbian/Gay Freedom Day with parade and rally.

Gay/Lesbian Pride Parade, Rally, and Festival in St. Louis. Write: St. Louis Lesbian and Gay Pride Celebration Committee, PO Box 23260, St. Louis MO 63156; call: 314-776-7138.

Chicago's Gay and Lesbian Pride Parade and Rally through the city's New Town area. Write: Chicago Gay & Lesbian Pride Week Planning Committee; PO Box 14131, Chicago IL 60614; 312-348-8243.

Transport to New York City's Gay/Lesbian Pride Parade by bus from Wilmington, Del. Write: Gay and Lesbian Alliance of Delaware, 214 Market St., Wilmington DE 19801; call: 302-655-5280.

June 25

B.A.S.I.C. bowling tournament in New York City. Call: 212-873-0154.

June 26

The Great Gay Race, sponsored by Lambda Car Clubs, concludes in Detroit. The winner is the car with the best distance/time factor, coming to Detroit from home and traveling within local speed limits. For application, write: Lambda Car Club, 1764 Rhoda Ave., Columbus OH 43212-1465; call: 614-486-0927.

June 27

Lambda Car Club National Invitational for antique auto fanciers begins in Dearborn, Mich., through June 30, and includes a banquet at the late Henry Ford's house, Fairlane. Write: Lambda Car Club, 1764 Rhoda Ave., Columbus OH 43212-1465; call: 614-486-0927.

June 29

Rocky Mountain Regional Rodeo begins in Denver, Colo., and continues through the July 4 weekend, with traditional rodeo events, such as calf roping and horse riding competitions. Write: Colorado Gay Rodeo Assn., 900 E. Colfax Ave., Denver CO 80218; phone: 303-839-8810.

Midwest Regional Conference of the World Congress of Gay and Lesbian Jewish Organizations begins in Toronto, Canada, and continues through July 1. This first regional meeting to be held outside the United States will have the theme "Living with Diversity in the Lesbian & Gay Community." For further information, write: World Congress of Gay and Lesbian Jewish Organizations, PO Box 18961, Washington DC 20036., or the sponsoring organization, CHUTZPAH, (the Toronto group for Jewish Lesbian and Gay men), PO Box 6103 Station A, Toronto, Ontario, Canada, M5W 1P5; call: 416-323 3564.

Liberty Belle Invitational Bowling Tournament in Philadelphia begins and continues through July 1. Call: 215-676-5665, 736-9433.

Women's Fourth of July Canoe Fest in Minnesota's Boundary Waters begins and continues through July 4. Write: Woodswomen, 25 W. Diamond Lake Rd., Minneapolis MN 55419; phone: 612-822-3809.

June 30

All Gay Cruise to French Canada, by RSVP Travel Productions, begins and continues through July 7 aboard the SS *Bermuda Star.* Ports of call along the St. Lawrence Seaway and the Atlantic coast include Montreal, Quebec City, and Provincetown, Mass. To book, call 303-467-7117 for the name of your local member of the International Gay Travel Assn. Or write: IGTA, PO Box 18247, Denver CO 80218.

San Diego Open V tennis tournament begins and continues through July 2 at San Diego State University, with open, B, C, and over 35's singles and doubles. About 140 players are expected to attend this warm-up for Gay Games III sponsored by the San Diego Tennis Federation, PO Box 33531, San Diego CA 92103; phone: 619-692-4274.

Golden Fleece Run XIX, in Colorado, sponsored by the Rocky Mountaineers Motorcycle Club on the club's own property near Fairplay, Colo., through July 4. Write: Rocky Mountaineers Motorcycle Club, PO Box 2629, Denver CO 80206; call: 303-733-7047.

To Be Announced

Fourstates Community AIDS Project Annual Meeting of all area supporters, members, PWAs, and HIV-affected people. For exact date and place, write: FSCAP, PO Box 3476, Joplin MO 64803-3476; call: 417-624-1250.

"You Must Remember This III," an entertaining, provocative, and moving reading of oral histories by gay and lesbian senior citizens. Sponsored by Seniors Active in a Gay Environment (SAGE), 208 W. 13th St., New York City, NY 10011; call: 212-741-2247.

Georgetown University Gay and Lesbian Alumni Assn. President's Reception. Write GALA-GU, PO Box 66094, Washington DC 20035.

American Gay Atheists of New York Pride Week meetings and parties. For more information, write: AGA New York, PO Box 248 Village Sta., New York NY 10014; call: 718-899-1737.

Canoe Trip for Women of all ages through the Canadian Wilderness, some quiet water, some white water. Instruction, equipment, and food provided. Write: Women in the Wilderness, 566 Ottawa Ave., St. Paul MN 55107; call: 612-227

River Rafting Weekend, sponsored by Colorado Outdoor & Ski Assn.,

PO Box 18598, Denver CO ; call: 303-470-9658.

Fifth Anniversary Reading and Celebration of *Evergreen Chronicles: A Journal of Gay and Lesbian Writers*. Event will coincide with the Twin Cities gay/lesbian pride festivities. For exact date and place. Write: Evergreen Chronicles, PO Box 8939, Minneapolis MN 55408.

Square Dance Fly-In In Philadelphia. Write: Independence Squares, 48 Bayard St. Rear Apt., Trenton NJ 08611; call: 609-394-1371.

Whitewater Rafting Trip for gays and lesbians floats through the heart of California's Gold Rush country. Transportation from Long Beach, Calif., meals, two days of rafting, and camping included. Write: The Gay and Lesbian Center of Long Beach, 2017 E. 4th St., Long Beach CA 90814; call: 213-434-4455.

Gay Pride Picnic in Carpenter State Park, Newark, N.J., bring your own food. Contact: Gay & Lesbian Alliance of Delaware, 214 N. Market St., Wilmington DE 19801; 302-655-5280.

Concert in Ft. Lauderdale, Fla., at the Parker Play House, by the Gay Men's Chorus of South Florida, 12555 Biscayne Blvd., Miami FL 33181-2597; call: 305-757-7464.

Pride Parade and Festival in West Hollywood, one of the nation's largest, sponsored by Christopher Street West. For exact date and details, call: 213-656-6553.

Pride Concert In Honolulu, tentatively planned for June. Write: Honolulu Men's Chorus, PO Box 4076, Honolulu HI 96812; call: 808-263-0910.

Seventh Anniversary Celebration of Christ the Redeemer Metropolitan Community Church in Evanston, Ill. Write: PO Box 6146 Evanston IL 60204

National Women's Music Festival may be held in Bloomington, Ind., in late May or in June. Write: PO Box 1568, Bloomington IN 47402.

Key West International Gay Film Festival held in Key West, Fla. For information about exact dates, write: The Key West Business Guild, Inc., 612 Fleming St., Key West FL 33040.

If Your Organization's Events Are Not Listed...

It's because we did not know about them. Remedy this situation for next year by sending us a list of your group's 1991 events. Just mail them to:

ENVOY ENTERPRISES
740 N. Rush St., Suite 609
Chicago IL 60611

Sun	Mon	Tues	Wed	Thur	Fri	Sat
1	2	3	4	5	6	7
8	9	10	11	12	13	14
15	16	17	18	19	20	21
22	23	24	25	26	27	28
29	30	31				

July 1

Women's Windjammer Cruise aboard the Yankee Clipper, sets sail from Antigua for a six-night "Seascape" cruise, starting at $975 per person. To book, call 303-467-7117 for the name of your local member of the International Gay Travel Assn. Or write: IGTA, PO Box 18247, Denver CO 80218.

July 4

Not to be held: Northwest Gay/Lesbian Sports Festival. This event, sponsored by Team Seattle, will not be held this year because of preparations for the August Gay Games III in Vancouver. It will be held again in 1991. Write: Team Seattle, 1206 E. Pike #515, Seattle WA 98122; call: 206-322-2777.

Dance at Nomad Village, Bethany Beach, Del., over the holiday weekend to benefit the Gay and Lesbian Alliance of Delaware. $3.00 at the door, gifts for the first 100 people. For exact date, write: GLAD, 214 Market St., Wilmington DE 19801; call: 302-655-5280.

Fireworks Boat Cruise, "Load the Boat II," and dancing on the river in New York City. Write: Times Squares, PO Box 1229 Ansonia Station, New York NY 10023.

July 6

Gay/Lesbian trip to Yosemite National Park departs from Long Beach for two nights at Curry Village private cabins and a tour of the park, hiking, and beautiful day and night vistas on this full-moon weekend. Write: The Gay and Lesbian Center of Long Beach, 2017 E. 4th St., Long Beach CA 90814; call: 213-434-4455.

July 7

Mountaineering Trip for Women in Washington's Cascade Mountains begins and continues through June 8. Write: Woodswomen, 25 W. Diamond Lake Rd., Minneapolis MN 55419; phone: 612-822-3809.

July 11

Intermediate Women's Rock Climbing Weekend in Washington State through July 12. Write: Woodswomen, 25 W. Diamond Lake Rd., Minneapolis MN 55419; phone: 612-822-3809.

July 14

Women's Learn to Canoe Weekend. Write: Woodswomen, 25 W. Diamond Lake Rd., Minneapolis MN 55419; phone: 612-822-3809.

Concert in Los Angeles by the Gay Men's Chorus of Los Angeles, 8:00 p.m. at the Embassy Theater, 851 S. Grand Ave. For ticket information, write the chorus at 7985 Santa Monica Blvd. #109-134, West Hollywood, CA 90046; phone: 213-462-5284.

July 15

Concert in Los Angeles, repeated at 4:00 p.m. See July 14 listing.

Women's Canoe Trip through the Boundary Waters of Minnesota through July 21. Write: Woodswomen, 25 W. Diamond Lake Rd., Minneapolis MN 55419; phone: 612-822-3809.

Glacier Travel and Ice Climbing for Women through July 21 in Washington State. Write: Woodswomen, 25 W. Diamond Lake Rd., Minneapolis MN 55419; phone: 612-822-3809.

Women's Trip to Brittany, France, begins and continues through July 29, with bicycling and general exploring of the area. Write: Woodswomen, 25 W. Diamond Lake Rd., Minneapolis MN 55419; phone: 612-822-3809.

July 18

Third International Lesbian and Gay Health Conference and Eighth National AIDS Forum begins at the Washington Hilton in Washington, DC, and continues through July 22, with an expected 1,500 attendees. The theme is "Developing Stronger Networks," among individuals and the community to meet the next decade's needs. Write: NLGHF, 1638 R. St., NW, Suite 2, Washington DC 20009; call: 202-797-3708.

July 19

Women's Bicycle Tour of Nova Scotia sets off for 14 days of traveling scenic and historic trails in Canada's Atlantic Ocean playground. Write: Womantrek, 1411 E. Olive Way, PO Box 20643, Seattle WA 98102; call: 206-325-4772.

July 20

Gaylaxicon '90, a science fiction convention for gay people and their friends, begins in Tewksbury, Mass., continuing through July 22 with guest of honor Melissa Scott and artist guest of honor Hannah Shapiro. Write: The Gaylaxians, PO Box 1051, Back Bay Annex, Boston MA 02117.

International Gay Rodeo Convention begins in Wichita, Kansas, and continues through July 22. New officers will be elected. Write: Colorado Gay Rodeo Assn., 900 E. Colfax Ave., Denver CO 80218; phone: 303-839-8810.

Sunshine Invitational Bowling Tournament in Orlando, Fla. Call: 407-897-3139.

July 21

Llama Pack Trip For Women to the Eagle Cap Wilderness of northern Oregon begins and continues through July 28. Easy pace--four to seven miles per day. Write: Womantrek, 1411 E. Olive Way, PO Box 20643, Seattle WA 98102; call: 206-325-4772.

Beach Trip for Car Lovers in Oregon, sponsored by the Northwest Scenic Cruisers, 206-254-1995.

July 22

Women's African Safari leaves for a tour featuring interactions with people as well as wildlife and sightseeing, through August 13. All women welcome, not limited to lesbians. Write: Womantrek, 1411 E. Olive Way, PO Box 20643, Seattle WA 98102; call: 206-325-4772.

Women's Mountaineering Trip over the Ptarmigan Transverse begins and continues through July 28. Write: Woodswomen, 25 W. Diamond Lake Rd., Minneapolis MN 55419; phone: 612-822-3809.

July 28

Annual Run of the Barbary Coaster's Motorcycle Club at Kenton Mine Lodge, about four hours north of San Francisco. For more information about this week-end outing and camping trip, write: Barbary Coaster's Motorcycle Club, PO Box 14251. San Francisco CA 94114-0251; call: 415-255-9865.

Annual Swim Party and Pot Luck Barbeque sponsored by Girth and Mirth of Greater San Francisco, PO Box 528, San Francisco CA 94101; Events subject to change, so call the 24- Hour Hot Line: 415-552-1143.

Geoduck Square Dance Fly-In in Seattle, just prior to Gay Games III in Vancouver, hosted by the Puddletown Squares, PO Box 20671, Seattle WA 98102; phone: 206-324-8786.

Women's Tour of China to the Yangste River Valley and Beijing, Xi'an, Nanjing, Shanghai, Guilin, begins and continues through August 21. All women welcome, not limited to lesbians. Write: Womantrek, 1411 E. Olive Way, PO Box 20643, Seattle WA 98102; call: 206-325-4772.

Canoe Trip for Women Over 40 begins and continues through August 8 in Minnesota's Boundary Waters. Write: Woodswomen, 25 W. Diamond Lake Rd., Minneapolis MN 55419; phone: 612-822-3809.

July 29

Backpacking Trip for Women to Mt. Olympus begins and continues through August 4. Write: Woodswomen, 25 W. Diamond Lake Rd., Minneapolis MN 55419; phone: 612-822-3809.

To Be Announced

New Year's in July, resort weekend in the Saugatuck/Douglas area of Michigan. Write: Douglas Dunes, PO Box 369, Douglas MI 49406; call: 616-857-1401.

Lake Powell Trip and Hot Springs Weekend for gays and lesbians. Write: Colorado Outdoor & Ski Assn., PO Box 18598, Denver CO ; call: 303-470-9658.

Square Dance Fly-In in Denver planned for late July or early August, sponsored by the Rocky Mountain Rainbeaus, 1519 S. Sherman St., Denver CO 80210; phone: 303-778-1937.

Dancing in the Street Celebration in Cleveland, sponsored by the Cleveland City Country Dancers, PO Box 14276, Cleveland OH 44114-0276; phone: 216-574-2203.

Whitewater Rafting Trip for gays and lesbians with camping at river's edge. Write: The Gay and Lesbian Center of Long Beach, 2017 E. 4th St., Long Beach CA 90814; call: 213-434-4455.

Picnic for Wimmin Only near Kalamazoo, Mich. Dinner and games. For details, write: Lavender Morning, PO Box 729, Kalamazoo MI 49005, phone: 616-685-5377.

Emerald City Invitational V Bowling Tournament in Seattle, Wash. Call: 206-725-3211; or 285-5657.

Annual West Coast Meet for Antique Car Lovers. For dates and place, call the Northwest Scenic Cruisers, 206-254-1995.

Moonlight Cruise on the Delaware River aboard the Spirit of Philadelphia, for 700, with prizes and surprises. Write: Liberty Belle Invitational, 248 South 11th St., Philadelphia PA 19107, call: 215-981-0807.

WARNING!

The Date of Any Event Can Change

Even gay/lesbian pride parade days have been known to change.

So take no chances. Before you get your heart set on attending an event--and especially if you need to travel to get there–check it out with the sponsoring organization.

Call or write them to be sure the date has not been changed.

Sun	Mon	Tues	Wed	Thur	Fri	Sat
			1	2	3	4
5	6	7	8	9	10	11
12	13	14	15	16	17	18
19	20	21	22	23	24	25
26	27	28	29	30	31	

August 2

Gay/Lesbian Rights Booth opens at the Ohio State Fair, through August 19, to provide information about statewide gay/lesbian organizations, distribute educational materials, bumperstickers, and buttons. Write: Stonewall Union, PO Box 10814, Columbus OH 43201-7814. phone: 614-299-7764.

August 3

Maple Leaf Classic VII Bowling Tournament begins in Toronto, Canada, and continues through August 5. Call: 416-465-0624.

San Diego Invitational Bowling Tournament begins and continues through August 5.

August 4

Celebration 90: Gay Games III and Cultural Festival begins in Vancouver and continues through August 11. For full details, see the Gay Games Section begining on page 7.

HOTLANTA RIVER EXPO in Atlanta, Ga., features a weekend of parties, the National Mr. Hotlanta Contest, a dance for 4,000, and a hilarious rafting trip down the Chattahoochee River. For details, write: Hotlanta, PO Box 8528, Atlanta GA 30308; or call: 404-874-3976.

August 5

Backpacking Trip for Women to Mt. Rainier begins and continues through August 11. Write: Woodswomen, 25 W. Diamond Lake Rd., Minneapolis MN 55419; phone: 612-822-3809.

August 6

Swiss Alps Hiking Trip for Women begins and continues through August 19. Write: Woodswomen, 25 W. Diamond Lake Rd., Minneapolis MN 55419; phone: 612-822-3809.

Women's Canoe Trip exploring the Quetico Canoe Country begins and continues through August 19. Write: Woodswomen, 25 W. Diamond Lake Rd., Minneapolis MN 55419; phone: 612-822-3809.

August 7

Women's Rafting Adventure on the Main Salmon River in Idaho shoves off for 6 days of floating, camping, and soaking in natural hot springs. Write: Womantrek, 1411 E. Olive Way, PO Box 20643, Seattle WA 98102; call: 206-325-4772.

August 8

Michigan Womyn's Music Festival begins and continues though August 12 on land near Hart, Mich., featuring music by women performers, workshops, crafts, camping, and the company of thousands of lesbians. Write: PO Box 22, Walhala MI 49458; or call: 616-757-4766.

August 11

Beginning Women's Rock Climbing Weekend in Washington State through August 19. Write: Woodswomen, 25 W. Diamond Lake Rd., Minneapolis MN 55419; phone: 612-822-3809.

River Trip in Oregon, the Annual Fruit Float on the McKenzie River sponsored by MCC Eugene. Rafts, inner tubes, and floats leave at 11 am for a day of fun. The evening will end with a dance and dinner. For details, write: Metropolitan Community Church of Eugene, PO Box 10091, Eugene OR 97440; call: 503-345-5963.

August12

Canoe Trip for Book Club Fans of Minnesota begins and continues through August 18. Write: Woodswomen, 25 W. Diamond Lake Rd., Minneapolis MN 55419; phone: 612-822-3809.

Women's Mountaineering Trip in the Northwest begins and continues through August 25. Write: Woodswomen, 25 W. Diamond Lake Rd., Minneapolis MN 55419; phone: 612-822-3809.

Auto Rodeo in Oregon, the third annual, in fact. For place and other details, call the Northwest Scenic Cruisers at 206-254-1995.

August 13

Camp Camp-It-Up in Hawaii, begins a week of summer camp activities for gays and lesbians, including swimming at beach and waterfalls, nature walks, learning about native dance and art, entertainment, and personal development through August 19. For details, write: Kalani Honua Health & Beach Ranch, Box 4500, Pahoa-Kalapana, HI 96778; phone:808-965-7828.

August 18

Intermediate Women's Rock Climbing Weekend in Washington State through August 19. Write: Woodswomen, 25 W. Diamond Lake Rd., Minneapolis MN 55419; phone: 612-822-3809.

August 24

Third Gay Asian Conference begins in Bangkok, Thailand, and continues through August 26, with representatives from Japan, Thailand, Hong Kong, South Korea, Malaysia, and Singapore. Write: Teishire Minami, JILGA, 201 Hohyu Building 2-11-9, Yotsuya Shinjuku-ku, Tokyo 160, Japan.

August 25

Annual Russian River Trip and Dinner in Monte Rio, sponsored by Girth and Mirth of Greater San Francisco, PO Box 528, San Francisco CA 94101; Events subject to change, so call the 24- Hour Hot Line: 415-552-1143.

English Bay Round-Up Cruise, a three-hour boat cruise in Vancouver's English Bay hosted by Squares Across the Border, PO Box 4404 Main Post Office, Vancouver, B.C., CANADA V6B 3Z8. Call: 604-683-6008.

August 26

Gay Greek Islands Cruise aboard the motor-sailer *Elina,* for 24 people. To book, call 303-467-7117 for the name of your local member of the International Gay Travel Assn. Or write: IGTA, PO Box 18247, Denver CO 80218.

August 30

West Coast Women's Music & Comedy Festival begins and continues through September 3 at a private campground at the base of Yosemite, Calif. Workshops, swimming, crafts, dances, sports. Camping, cabins, and R.V.s. Write: Robin Tyler Productions, 15842 Chase St., Sepulveda CA 91343; Phone: 818-893-4075.

To Be Announced

Fourstates Community AIDS Project Advisory Board Meeting with the local medical community and social service representatives. For exact date and place, write: FSCAP, PO Box 3476, Joplin MO 64803-3476; call: 417-624-1250.

Annual Retreat of the Arkansas Gay and Lesbian Task Force. For particulars, write: AGLTF, PO Box 45053, Little Rock AR 72214; or call: 501-663-3340.

Box Lunch Auction and Picnic in Huntsville, Ala., with volleyball, swimming, games, and a crafts and services auction. Write: Metropolitan Community Church of Huntsville, PO Box 10021, Huntsville AL 35801; call: 205-533-6220.

Whitewater Rafting Trip for gays and lesbians in California, with camping at river's edge. Write: The Gay and Lesbian Center of Long Beach, 2017 E. 4th St., Long Beach CA 90814; call: 213-434-4455.

Demonstration Square Dancing in Chicago at Halsted St. Market Days, by the Chi-Town Squares, PO Box 14897, Chicago IL 60614; call: 312-549-5698.

Moonlight Cruise on the Delaware River aboard the Spirit of Philadelphia, for 700, with prizes and surprises. Write: Liberty Belle Invitational, 248 South 11th St., Philadelphia PA 19107, call: 215-981-0807.

September

Sun	Mon	Tues	Wed	Thur	Fri	Sat
						1
2	3	4	5	6	7	8
9	10	11	12	13	14	15
16	17	18	19	20	21	22
23	24	25	26	27	28	29
30						

Gay/Lesbian Square Dance Month,

sponsored by the International Association of Gay Square Dance Clubs, to promote awareness of the activities of the international association and its member clubs. For more information on how to join or start a club, call: 415-431-6272.

September 1

Hoedown in Seattle over the Labor Day Weekend, sponsored by the Puddletown Squares, PO Box 20671, Seattle WA 98102; Call 206-324-8786.

Dance at Nomad Village, Bethany Beach, Del., over the holiday weekend to benefit the Gay and Lesbian Alliance of Delaware. $3.00 at the door, gifts for the first 100 people. For exact date, write: GLAD, 214 Market St., Wilmington DE 19801; call: 302-655-5280.

Joint Anniversary Celebration of Louisville and Indianapolis Chapters of Black and White Men Together, through September 3. Write: BWMT, 8303 W. 21st St., Indianapolis IN 46234.

September 2

Gay Greek Islands Cruise aboard the 40-passenger motor yacht *Double Force* departs for seven days, starting at $1549 per person. To book, call 303-467-7117 for the name of your local member of the International Gay Travel Assn. Or write: IGTA, PO Box 18247, Denver CO 80218.

September 3

Llama Pack Trip For Women to the Eagle Cap Wilderness of northern Oregon through September 8. Write: Womantrek, 1411 E. Olive Way, PO Box 20643, Seattle WA 98102; call: 206-325-4772.

September 6

Annual Membership Meeting and political candidates' night of Stonewall Union in Columbus, Ohio, PO Box 10814, Columbus OH 43201-7814; phone: 614-299-7764.

September 7

Women's Trek on the Isle of Crete to savor ancient sites of Greek and Minoan culture through September 23. Write: Womantrek, 1411 E. Olive Way, PO Box 20643, Seattle WA 98102; call: 206-325-4772.

San Diego Gay Rodeo begins and continues through September 10, with horse events, wild-bull riding, calf roping, and steer decorating. For ticket information, write: Golden State Gay Rodeo Assn., PO Box 691865, Los Angeles, CA 90069; call: 213-498-1675.

September 8

Beginning Women's Rock Climbing Weekend in Washington State through September 9. Write: Woodswomen, 25 W. Diamond Lake Rd., Minneapolis MN 55419; phone: 612-822-3809.

Strike Against AIDS Bowling Tournament in Chicago , continues on September 15 and 16. Call: 312-935-7317.

September 9

Women's Leadership Course in the Pacific Northwest begins and continues through September 16. Cost: $640. Write: Woodswomen, 25 W. Diamond Lake Rd., Minneapolis MN 55419; phone: 612-822-3809.

Annual Autumn Canoe Trip for Women through the Minnesota Boundary Waters. Write: Woodswomen, 25 W. Diamond Lake Rd., Minneapolis MN 55419; phone: 612-822-3809.

September 15

Coronation of the Grand Duke and Grand Duchess in San Francisco at the Cathedral Hill Hotel for a one-year reign. For information, write: The Council of Grand Dukes and Grand Duchesses, 2261 Market St., Box 402, San Francisco CA 94114-1693; call: 415-255-9865.

Concourse dé Not so Elegant for antique car buffs in Oregon, sponsored by the Northwest Scenic Cruisers, 206-254-1995.

Fall Meeting of Affirmation/United Methodists begins and continues through September 16. For the location, write them at PO Box 1021, Evanston IL 60204; phone: 312-475-0499.

September 21

Rosh Hashanah. Many gay/lesbian Jewish groups hold services. For a listing of names and addresses, see page 96.

High Holy Day Services : Congregation Etz Chaim, 19094 W. Dixie Hwy., North Miami Beach FL 33180; call: 305-931-9318.

September 22

End of Summer Swim Party and Pot Luck Dinner sponsored by Girth and Mirth of Greater San Francisco, PO Box 528, San Francisco CA 94101; Events subject to change, so call the 24- Hour Hot Line: 415-552-1143.

Intermediate Women's Rock Climbing Weekend in Washington State through September 23. Write: Woodswomen, 25 W. Diamond Lake Rd., Minneapolis MN 55419; phone: 612-822-3809.

September 23

"From All Walks of Life," the Third Annual 10k Pledge Walk to fight AIDS, enlists the feet of up to 4,000 walkers through several Denver city parks in the largest fund-raiser for AIDS service providers in Colorado. Write: Colorado AIDS Project, 1576 Sherman St., Denver CO 80203; call: 303-837-0166.

September 29

Kolnidre: Congregation Etz Chaim, 19094 W. Dixie Hwy., North Miami Beach FL 33180; call: 305-931-9318.

September 30

Yom Kippur service: Congregation Etz Chaim, 19094 W. Dixie Hwy., North Miami Beach FL 33180; call: 305-931-9318.

Other Jewish groups may hold services. See page 96.

To Be Announced

Annual Stonewall Awards Dinner in Columbus, Ohio., honoring local gays and lesbians at a gala dinner/dance. Write: Stonewall Union, PO Box 10814, Columbus OH 10814; call: 614-299-7764.

Georgetown University Gay and Lesbian Alumni Assn. Welcome Back Party. Write GALA-GU, PO Box 66094, Washington DC 20035.

Indoor Camp Meeting in Grand Rapids, Mich., featuring quest speakers Rev. Dolores P. Berry and Rev. Elder Freda Smith of the Universal Fellowship of Metropolitan Community Churches. Sponsored by Reconciliation Metropolitan Community Church, PO Box 1259; Grand Rapids MI 49501; call: 616-364-7633.

Fourth Anniversary Show and Celebration of MCC Huntsville (Ala.) consists of a variety show or play and special worship service. Write: Metropolitan Community Church of Huntsville, PO Box 10021, Huntsville AL 35801; call: 205-533-6220.

Recruiting Dance for Square Dancers in Eureka, Calif., sponsored by the Sequoia Ocean Waves, 3370 F. St., Eureka, CA 95501; 707-444-2775.

Square Dance Fly-In, Crossfire II, in Chicago, hosted by the Chi-Town Squares, PO Box 14897, Chicago IL 60614; phone 312-549-5698.

The Gatsby, biggest party of the year in Long Beach, Calif., to raise funds for the Gay and Lesbian Center, with dinner, dancing, entertainment, and auctions at the Hyatt Regency at Shoreline Village. For exact date, write: The Gay and Lesbian Center of Long Beach, 2017 E. 4th St., Long Beach CA 90814; call: 213-434-4455.

Paul Bunyon Invitational Bowling Tournament in Minneapolis/St. Paul. Call: 612-646-1396.

Show Me Classic Bowling Tournament in St. Louis, Mo. Call: 314-771-2878, or 752-3108.

Showgirl Invitational Bowling Tournament in Las Vegas. Call: 702-361-6091

F.L.I.R.T. Bowling Tournament in Ft. Lauderdale, Fla. Call: 305-583-2548.

Motown Invitational Classic Bowling Tournament in Detroit. Call: 313-369-2083.

Convergence '90: Convention of Associated Big Men's Clubs in Chicago at the City Center Holiday Inn. Write PO Box 14384, Chicago IL 60614; phone: 312-776-9223.

Second Annual East Coast Lesbian Festival is tentatively scheduled for the Labor Day Weekend in western Massachusetts. For confirmation and reservations, call: 718-643-3284.

Folson St. Fair in San Francisco south of Market St., provides a showcase for gay/lesbian arts and crafts. Inquire with local merchants.

Sun	Mon	Tues	Wed	Thur	Fri	Sat
	1	2	3	4	5	6
7	8	9	10	11	12	13
14	15	16	17	18	19	20
21	22	23	24	25	26	27
28	29	30	31			

October 5

Homecoming Dance in Seattle on Friday and Saturday nights, sponsored by the Puddletown Squares, PO Box 20671, Seattle WA 98102; phone: 206-324-8786.

Anniversary, Washington, D.C., Chapter, Black and White Men Together continues through October 8. Write: BWMT, 1101 L St. NW #206, Washington DC 20005; phone: 202-371-1919.

October 11

National Coming Out Day. To encourage gays and lesbians to take one more step out of the closet. Write: PO Box 15524, Santa Fe NM 87506; phone: 505-982-2558.

October 12

Ninth International Convention of P.F.L.A.G. begins at the Hyatt Regency Hotel in Orange County, Calif., and continues through October 14. The convention of Parents and Friends of Lesbians and Gays provides for lesbians, gays, their parents and friends workshops focusing on loving and supporting our children, health, religion, legal issues, youth issues and family concerns. Banquet, entertainment, and dancing. Write: P.F.L.A.G., PO Box 28662, Santa Ana CA 9279908662; call: 714-998-5844.

October 13

Balloon Fiesta Gay Square Dance Festival begins in Albuquerque and continues through October 14. This square dance "fly-in" is held annually in conjunction with Albuquerque's colorful festival of hot-air balloons. Write: The Wilde Bunch, PO Box 40393, Albuquerque MN 87196; call: 505-255-2150.

October 17

Meeting of the General Council of the United Fellowship of Metropolitan Community Churches and UFMCC Great Lakes District Conference begins in Chicago, culminating on October 20 with the 20th Anniversary Celebration of Good Shepherd Parish MCC. Write: UFMCC Great Lakes District, PO Box 5757, Dayton OH 45410; phone: 513-277-8815.

October 20

The 22nd Anniversary Celebration of the Rocky Mountaineers Motorcycle Club begins and continues through October 23 in Denver. Write: Rocky Mountaineers Motorcycle Club, PO Box 2629, Denver CO 80206; call: 303-733-7047.

October 26

Annual Conference of the Committee of Black Gay Men begins and continues through October 28 in Chicago. Write: CBGM, PO Box 7209, Chicago 60680; call: 312-248-5188.

All Gay Cruise by RSVP Travel Productions, "A Party to Remember," sails from Miami for a three-day Fantasy Fest at Sea, featuring a stop at Key West for that town's fabled Halloween Celebration. To book, call 303-467-7117 for the name of your local member of the International Gay Travel Assn. Or write: IGTA, PO Box 18247, Denver CO 80218.

Square Dance Fly-In in New York City begins and continues through October 28. Write: Times Squares, PO Box 1229 Ansonia Station, New York NY 10023.

First International Consortium on Lesbian and Gay Spirituality and Theology begins and continues through October 28 in Los Angeles, sponsored by the Institute of Gay/Lesbian Theology and Spirituality and Samaritan College, the Seminary of the United Fellowship of Metropolitan Community Churches. Write: Consortium Coordinator, 5879 Washington Blvd., Culver City CA 90232; call: 213-930-1600.

October 27

All Gay Fantasy Fest Cruise. See October 26 listing.

Annual Girth and Mirth Halloween Party in San Francisco, with NAAFA. For details, write: Girth and Mirth of Greater San Francisco, PO Box 528, San Francisco CA 94101; Events subject to change, so call the 24- Hour Hot Line: 415-552-1143.

Sock-Hop for Oregon's antique auto lovers, sponsored by the Northwest Scenic Cruisers, 206-254-1995.

October 28

Gay Windjammer Cruise departs from Grenada for six nights in the Caribbean, starting at $995. To book, call 303-467-7117 for the name of your local member of the International Gay Travel Assn. Or write: IGTA, PO Box 18247, Denver CO 80218.

Olivia Records Women's Cruise to the Caribbean sails from Miami and continues through Nov. 4, with stops in Nassau, San Juan, St. Thomas, St. John, and the private island of Blue Lagoon. Write: Olivia Reconds, 440 Market St., Oakland CA 94608; phone: 800-631-6277 or 415-655-0364.

October 31

Halloween Party in Los Angeles sponsored by The Dark Shadows Fan Club, gay fans of TV's Gothic soap opera. Write them at: PO Box 69A04, West Hollywood CA 90069; or call: 213-650-5112.

To Be Announced

First Annual Kamp Meeting Revival in Eugene Ore., an MCC gospel extravaganza with preachers, healers, and gospel singers from all over the Pacific Northwest. Write: MCC Eugene, PO Box 10091, Eugene OR 97440; call: 503-345-5963.

Second Annual Colorado Lesbian and Gay Congress, to review events of the past year and elect next year's steering committee. Write: Colorado Gay and Lesbian Task Force, PO Box 18632, Denver CO 80218; call: 303-830-2981.

Halloween Party in the very gay Saugatuck/Douglas area of Michigan at the Douglas Dunes resort motel. Write: Douglas Dunes, PO Box 369, Douglas MI 49406; call: 616-857-1401.

Halloween Dance at Stanford University in California for men and women, with live D.J., $3.00 admission, costume optional. Sponsored by the Lesbian, Gay, and Bisexual Community Center, PO Box 8265, Stanford CA 94309; call: 415-723-1488.

Halloween Dance in Atlanta, Ga., sponsored by the Dogwood City Dancers, PO Box 95522, Atlanta GA 30347; call: 404-237-2545 or 404-320-6408.

Halloween Dance in Cleveland, Ohio, sponsored by the Cleveland City Country Dancers, PO Box 14276, Cleveland OH 44114-0276; phone: 216-574-2203.

Harvest Dance for Wimmin Only in Kalamazoo, Mich., at the Peoples Church. Live band, munchies and coffee provided. BYOB. Write: Lavender Morning, PO Box 729, Kalamazoo MI 49005, phone: 616-685-5377.

Mid-Year International Gay Bowling Organization Meeting. Call: 214-526-8060 for date and place.

C.H.I.T. VIII Bowling Tournament in Washington D.C. Call: 202-332-5562 or 703-528-2145.

Women's Tour of Tibet, 2 weeks from Katmandu to Lhasa, has been tentatively planned. No hiking. For confirmation, write: Womantrek, 1411 E. Olive Way, PO Box 20643, Seattle WA 98102; call: 206-325-4772.

Annual Membership Conference of the North American Man/Boy Love Association. Contact NAMBLA, PO Box 174, New York NY 10018, call: 212-807-8578.

Women's Two-Week Tour of Russia has been tentatively planned. Write: Womantrek, 1411 E. Olive Way, PO Box 20643, Seattle WA 98102; call: 206-325-4772.

Women's Caribbean Flotilla is being planned, with six women per boat, for a week of sailing, snorkeling, swimming, and windsurfing. For confirmation, write: Womantrek, 1411 E. Olive Way, PO Box 20643, Seattle WA 98102; call: 206-325-4772.

Street Festival in West Hollywood, a very popular event with gays and lesbians, featuring blues, jazz, and rock bands, food and crafts booths. Write: City of West Hollywood, 8611 Santa Monica Blvd., West Hollywood CA 90069.

Halloween Party in West Hollywood, when the city closes part of Santa Monica Blvd., and turns it over to the outrageously costumed. Write: City of West Hollywood, 8611 Santa Monica Blvd., West Hollywood CA 90069.

International Gay Rodeo Finals. For exact date and location, write: Golden State Gay Rodeo Assn., PO Box 691865, Los Angeles CA 90069; phone: 213-498-1675.

Pioneer Days in Southern California, an old-fashioned fair in the San Fernando Valley. Write: Valley Business Alliance, PO Box 1157, Burbank CA 91507-1157; call: 818-760-3825 or 213-937-4553.

Halloween Weekend in Provincetown, Mass. Write: Provincetown Business Guild, PO Box 421, Provincetown MA 02657; 617-487-2313.

Conference on Gay and Lesbian Identity in Chicago, sponsored by Horizons Community Center, 3225 N. Sheffield, Chicago IL 60657; phone 312-929-4357.

Sun	Mon	Tues	Wed	Thur	Fri	Sat
				1	2	3
4	5	6	7	8	9	10
11	12	13	14	15	16	17
18	19	20	21	22	23	24
25	26	27	28	29	30	

November 9

Third Annual National Gay and Lesbian Task Force Conference, "Creating Change," begins in Minneapolis and continues through November 12, with exhibits, workshops, seminars, special speakers, and social events. For details, write: National Gay and Lesbian Task Force, 1517 U St. NW, Washington DC 20009; call: 202-332-6483.

November 10

Women's Trek Through Nepal begins, a moderate trek from Pokhara to the Annapurna Sanctuary, named for a goddess, surrounded by the Himalayan mountains. Sherpa guides and porters. Trip continues through December 1. Write: Womantrek, 1411 E. Olive Way, PO Box 20643, Seattle WA 98102; call: 206-325-4772.

November 16

Texas Gay Rodeo begins and continues through November 18, with horse events, wild-bull riding, calf roping, and steer decorating. For location, write: Texas Gay Rodeo Assn. PO Box 64904, Dallas TX 75206.

November 17

A Women's Cruise along the Mexican Riviera sets sail from San Diego with scheduled stops at Cabo San Lucas, Puerto Vallarta, and Mazatlan. Special on-board festivities include the Eleanor Roosevelt Reception, a Thanksgiving Day Feast, and the Alice B. Toklas/Gertrude Stein Formal Dinner-Dance. Write: Robin Tyler Productions, 15842 Chase St., Sepulveda CA 91343; call: 1-818-893-1593; FAX: 1-818-893-1593.

Progressive Thanksgiving Dinner in Oregon for antique car lovers. hosted by Northwest Scenic Cruisers, 206-254-1995.

November 21

Thanksgiving Fiesta trip to Mexico for four nights by Advance Travel. To book, call 303-467-7117 for the name of your local member of the International Gay Travel Assn. Or write: IGTA, PO Box 18247, Denver CO 80218.

November 22

Thanksgiving Dinner in Key West, Fla., with all the trimmings followed by a Worship Service. Write: Metropolitan Community Church Key West, 1215 Petronia St., Key West, FL 33040; call: 305-294-8912.

November 23

Seventh Anniversary Square Dance Fly-In in Vancouver runs through November 24, hosted by Squares Across the Border, PO Box 4404 Main Post Office, Vancouver, B.C., CANADA V6B 3Z8. Call: 604-683-6008. This date is somewhat tentative and subject to change. Be sure to call!

November 24

Thanksgiving Party in San Francisco, sponsored by Girth and Mirth of Greater San Francisco, PO Box 528, San Francisco CA 94101; Events subject to change, so call the 24- Hour Hot Line: 415-552-1143.

November 30

Women's Bicycle Tour of West Africa begins and continues through December 22, visiting remote villages, absorbing folklore, and lodging at simple hotels and village accommodations. Write: Womantrek, 1411 E. Olive Way, PO Box 20643, Seattle WA 98102; call: 206-325-4772.

To Be Announced

Beginners/"Never-Evers" Day for novice gay/lesbian skiers at Keystone ski area near Denver, Colorado. Write: Colorado Outdoor & Ski Assn., PO Box 18598, Denver CO ; call: 303-470-9658.

Square Dance Fly-In in Washington, D.C., hosted by D.C. Lambda Squares, 11842 Enid Dr., Potomac MD 20854; call: 301-983-8935.

M.A.G.I.C. Bowling Tournament in Dayton, Ohio. Call: 513-276-5443.

S.F.N.T.I.T. Bowling Tournament in San Francisco. Call: 415-282-6002, 495-7848, or 626-8559.

Sparkling City Invitational Bowling Tournament in Corpus Christi, Tex. Call: 512-854-4141.

H.I.T. XII Bowling Tournament in Milwaukee, Wisc. Call: 414-342-2494, or 672-8960.

United Valley Invitation Thanksgiving Bowling Tournament in Los Angeles, Calif. Call: 818-763-0151 or 768-7381, or 213-664-5880.

Anniversary, Cleveland Chapter, Black and White Men Together. Write: BWMT, 3236 Dellwood Rd., Cleveland Heights, OH 44118; phone: 216-371-4597.

Confirm the Date!

Never make plans to attend an event unless you check soon before that event is scheduled to happen.

Often, dates are changed.

So don't be disappointed. Check with the sponsoring organization before you get your plans too firm.

Sun	Mon	Tues	Wed	Thur	Fri	Sat
						1
2	3	4	5	6	7	8
9	10	11	12	13	14	15
16	17	18	19	20	21	22
23	24	25	26	27	28	29
30	31					

December 1

National AIDS Day and Annual AIDS Vigil of Prayer in Eugene, Ore., Workshops, religious services, and healing for those who are living with AIDS or ARC. Write: MCC Eugene, PO Box 10091, Eugene OR 97440; call: 503-345-5963.

Christmas Square Dance in Atlanta, Ga., by the Dogwood City Dancers, PO Box 95522, Atlanta GA 30347; Phone: 404-237-2545 or 404-320-6408.

December 2

Christmas Concert in Portland, Ore., by the Portland Gay Men's Chorus, two performances at the Portland Center for the Performing Arts. write: PO Box 3223, Portland OR 97208; call: 503-227-7907.

December 9

Holiday Concert in Denver by the Denver Gay Men's Chorus, to be repeated on December 10. These dates are tentative, so for confirmation, write: Denver Gay Men's Chorus, PO Box 6717, Denver CO 80202; phone: 303-331-2302.

December 15

Tenth Anniversary Celebration of Reconciliation Metropolitan Community Church, 300 Graceland NE, Grand Rapids, Mich. Write: Reconciliation MCC, PO Box 1259; Grand Rapids MI 49501; call: 616-364-7633.

Concert in Los Angeles by the Gay Men's Chorus of Los Angeles, 8:00 p.m. at the Embassy Theater, 851 S. Grand Ave. For ticket information, write the chorus at 7985 Santa Monica Blvd. #109-134, West Hollywood, CA 90046; phone: 213-462-5284.

December 16

Concert in Los Angeles, repeated at 4:00 p.m. See December 15 listing.

December 22

Christmas Party in San Francisco sponsored by Girth and Mirth of Greater San Francisco, PO Box 528, San Francisco CA 94101; Events subject to change, so call the 24- Hour Hot Line: 415-552-1143.

Christmas Party in Oregon for antique auto buffs, hosted by the Northwest Scenic Cruisers, 206-254-1995.

December 23

Christmas Potluck Supper in Huntsville, Ala. Write: Metropolitan Community Church of Huntsville, PO Box 10021, Huntsville AL 35801; call: 205-533-6220.

December 24

Caroling Service and Light Supper in Key West, Fla., followed by the 11:00 pm Christmas Eve Worship Service Write: Metropolitan Community Church Key West, 1215 Petronia St., Key West, FL 33040; call: 305-294-8912.

Choir Concert and Christmas Eve Service in Grand Rapids, Mich., at Reconciliation Metropolitan Community Church, 300 Graceland NE, Write: Reconciliation MCC, PO Box 1259; Grand Rapids MI 49501; call: 616-364-7633.

Christmas Eve Services are held at many Metropolitan Community Churches. For information, see list of UFMCC Districts on page 93.

December 25

Christmas Day Worship Service, 11:00 a.m., and Buffet Lunch in Key

West, Fla. Write: Metropolitan Community Church Key West, 1215 Petronia St., Key West, FL 33040; call: 305-294-8912.

December 31

New Year's Eve Party in San Francisco sponsored by Girth and Mirth of Greater San Francisco, PO Box 528, San Francisco CA 94101; Events subject to change, so call the 24- Hour Hot Line: 415-552-1143.

Women's New Year's Dance tentatively planned in San Francisco. Write: Bay Area Career Women, 22 New Montgomery St., Suite 606, San Francisco CA 94105; phone: 415-495-5393.

To Be Announced

Holiday Concerts are performed during December by many local Gay/Lesbian Choruses. For a listing by state, see page 51.

Georgetown University Gay and Lesbian Alumni Assn. Holiday Party. Write GALA-GU, PO Box 66094, Washington DC 20035.

Christmas Resort Weekend in the Saugatuck/Douglas area of Michigan. Write: Douglas Dunes, PO Box 369, Douglas MI 49406; call: 616-857-1401.

Ski Trips in Colorado: On-slope BBQ and Party at Loveland; "Noon to Moon" Day at Keystone; both sponsored by: Colorado Outdoor & Ski Assn., PO Box 18598, Denver CO ; call: 303-470-9658.

Holiday Concert by the Gay Men's Chorus of Washington D.C., featuring secular selection for the Holiday season. Write: Gay Men's Chorus of Washington, PO Box 57043, Washington DC 20037; call: 202-338-SING.

Christmas Square Dance in Cleveland, Ohio. For details, write: Cleveland City Country Dancers, PO Box 14276, Cleveland OH 44114-0276; phone: 216-574-2203.

Fourth Annual San Francisco AIDS Dance-a-Thon, a major fundraiser for local AIDS support and action groups. Participants garner monetary pledges for each hour danced. For the date and all the details, contact: Mobilization Against AIDS, 1540 Market St., Suite 60, San Francisco CA 94102; or call: 415-863-4676.

Holiday Concerts in Chicago by the Windy City Gay Chorus (312-404-9242) and the Chicago Gay Men's Chorus (PO Box 14146, Chicago IL 60614; 312-477-9380).

Holiday Concert in Philadelphia by the Philadelphia Gay Men's Chorus, PO Box 58842, Philadelphia PA 19102; call: 215-732-5079.

Christmas Square Dance in New York City sometime in mid-December. Write: Times Squares, PO Box 1229 Ansonia Station, New York NY 10023.

Christmas Concert in Honolulu tentatively planned by the Honolulu Men's Chorus, PO Box 4076, Honolulu HI 96812; 808-263-0910.

1990 EVENTS TO BE ANNOUNCED

Dates for these events had not been set at the time we went to press

ANTIQUE AUTO MEETS

Local car clubs hold antique auto meets in various areas of the United States. For information, contact:

International, PO Box 12393, Columbus OH 43212; phone: 614-263-3673

Buckeye Region (Ohio), PO Box 12393, Columbus OH 43212; phone: 614-263-3673.

Delaware Valley Region, 11002 Kelvin, Philadelphia, PA 19116; phone: 215-638-4829.

Detroit Region, 23072 Beech St., Dearborn MI 48124; phone: 313-563-5824.

Dogwood Region (Georgia), PO Box 14665, Atlanta GA 30324; phone: 404-454-6423.

Florida Region, PO Box 12393, Columbus OH 43212; phone: 407-391-5752.

Hoosier Region, (Indiana), 230 E. 47th St., Indianapolis IN 46205; phone: 317-923-5803.

Lake Michigan Region (Ill. Wisc.), PO Box 268534, Chicago IL 60626; 312-973-7453.

Mississippi Region, 453 Pimlico Place, Jackson MS 39211; phone: 601-956-7933.

National Capital Region (Washington DC), 7302 Maple Ave., Takoma Park MD 20912, phone: 301-270-4876

North New England Region, 25 Downing St., Concord NH 03301; 603-224-2867.

New Mexico Region, 1902 Louise SW, Albuquerque NM 87105; phone: 505-873-3310.

New York Metro Region, 25 Clearview Ave., Selden NY 11784; phone: 516-698-0184.

Nutmeg Region (Connecticut), PO Box 1174, Avon CT 06001; phone: 203-673-0100

Tidewater Region (Norflok, Va.), 1854 East Ocean View Ave., Norfolk, VA 23503; phone: 804-583-3481.

Toronto Region, 50 Graydonhall Dr. #1903, Don Mills, Ont., Canada M3A 3A5; phone: 416- 391-0407.

Great Autos of Yesteryear holds meets in southern California. For dates, write: PO Box 4, Yorba Linda CA 92686.

Freewheelers Car Club hold meets in northern California. Write them at: 7 William Court, Sausalito CA 94965.

Ethyl Forever Car Club holds meets in the Pacific Northwest. For details, write: PO Box 2262, Seattle WA 98111.

Classic Chassis Car Club hold meets in Texas. Write: PO Box 12553, Austin TX 78711.

Classic Chassis Car Club of San Antonio, PO Box 33654, San Antonio TX 78233.

COMMUNITY EVENTS

Award dinners for and readings of published works about AIDS. Events are usually held on the West Coast, but this is a national organization. Write: Words Project for AIDS, PO Box 691133, Los Angeles CA 90069.

CONTESTS

California State Preliminary Contests for California Gay/Lesbian State Pageants:

Ms. California Lady-of-the Year (Lesbian)

Mr. Gay California All-American (Male)

Ms. Gay California/America (Female impersonator)

Write: Lettuce Entertainment Co, c/o Doug Christoff, 1008 Tenth St., Suite 364, Sacramento CA 95814; phone: 916-448-8656.

Fifth National Ms. Lady-of-the-Year Contest; Sixth National Mr. Gay All-American Contest, 18th National Miss Gay America Competition. Write: National Pageant Office, Norma Kristie, Inc., Little Rock AR 72214; call: 501-666-6900.

HOBBY GROUPS

Spring stamp show in New York City's Madison Square Garden. Gay

& Lesbian History on Stamps Club meets for brunch. Write: G & L History on Stamps Club, c/o Ed. S. Centeno, PO Box 3940, Hartford CT 06103.

Fall stamp show with exhibits of interest to gay.lesbian philatelists in New York City's Madison Square Garden. See address above.

PROFESSIONAL ASSOCIATIONS

Meeting of the Assn. of Gay and Lesbian Psychiatrists in Washington DC. For details, write them at 1732 S.E. Ash, Portland OR 97214.

Annual meeting of the Assn. of Lesbian and Gay Psychologists in Boston, in conjunction with the American Psychological Assn. convention.

Gay Public Health Workers Caucus annual meeting. Write: c/o C. Harris, 1417 Ames Pl. NE, Washington DC 20002; call: 202-543-1953.

RELIGIOUS GROUPS

Semi-annual gatherings of the Jewish Lesbian Daughters of Holocaust Survivors, usually at an East Coast location. For dates and places, write: PO Box 6194, Boston MA 02114; call: 617-321-4254.

Third Western Regional Conference of Gay and Lesbian Jews in Seattle and the Fourth Northeast Regional Conference of Gay and Lesbian Jews at a location to be announced. For dates, write: World Congress of Gay and Lesbian Jewish Organizations, PO Box 18961, Washington DC 20036.

East and West Regional Conferences of Presbyterians for Lesbian and Gay Concerns. Write: PO Box 38, New Brunswick NJ 08903-0038; call: 201-846-1510.

SQUARE DANCE EVENTS

Autumn Dance Workshops in Sacramento, Calif., co-hosted by the Prime 8's and the Capital City Squares. Write: Capital City Squares, PO Box 19986, Sacramento CA 95819; phone: 916-969-5153.

Camping and square dancing retreat in the fall sponsored by the Western Star Dancers, 584 Castro St., Suite 480, San Francisco CA 94114; phone: 415-864-6134 or 415-621-0862.

Square Dance Fly-In in Toronto planned for late spring or early summer. Contact: Triangle Squares, 28 Sackville Pl., Toronto, Ontario, M4X 1A4 Canada; 416-960-5458.

Spring Dance in Atlanta, sponsored by the Dogwood City Dancers, PO Box 95522, Atlanta GA 30347; 404-237-2545 or 404-320-6408.

Square Dance Fly-In in Atlanta. For information, see address above.

Barn Dance in New York City area planned for the spring. Write: Times Squares, PO Box 1229 Ansonia Station, New York NY 10023.

TOURS AND TRIPS

Adventure Travel for Men to Costa Rica's National Parks, Macchu Pichu, and Nepal. Write: Adventure Bound, 711 Walnut St., Carriage House, Boulder CO 80302; phone: 303-449-0990.

WOMEN'S GATHERINGS

Old Lesbians Organizing Committee forming to discuss a national political agenda for lesbians 60 years and older. For information write: OLOC, PO Box 14066, Chicago IL 60614; call: 312-477-5269.

Sisterfire, women's festival, may be held in the Washington DC area. Write: Sisterfire, 1475 Harvard St, NW, Washington DC 20009.

Lesbian Dance in Chicago sponsored by Horizons Community Services, 3225 N. Sheffield, Chicago IL 60657; 312-929-4357.

Index of Events

See date listed for information

ALUMNAE and STUDENTS ACTVITIES

Georgetown U.Alums, June tba, Sept. tba
Mt Holyoke College Al - ums, May 26,
NetGALA, TBA
Stanford U. Student Events, Feb. tba, May 1, Oct. tba

ANTIQUE AUTOS

Auto Meets, TBA
Great Gay Race, Dearborn, Jun 27,
Detroit, Jun 26,
Oregon (Northwest Scenic Cruisers, Jan 20 , Nov 17, Feb 24, Mar 17 , Apr 6 , May 15, Aug 12, Sep 15, July, tba

BOWLING

Seal Beach CAJan 13
Miami, Jan 13,
New York, Feb 13,
San Antonio, Feb 16
Tampa, Feb 16,
Phoenix Feb 16
Louisville, Feb 9
Vancouver , BC, Mar 16
Pittsburgh, Mar 30
Ft. Lauderdale, Mar 9
Calgary, Apr 12
Atlanta, Apr 13
Kansas City, Apr 13
Garden Grove, CA, Apr 20
Rochester NY, Apr 21,
Madison WI, Apr 21
Los Angeles, May 24
New York City, May 4
Portland OR, Jun 2
Chicago, Jun 22, Sept. 8
New York City, Jun 25
Philadelphia, Jun 29
Cleveland, Jun 8
Orlando, Jul 20
Toronto, Aug 3
San Diego, Aug 3
Seattle, July tba
San Jose CA, Mar tba
Dayton, Nov tba
Milwaukee, Nov. tba
San Francisco, Nov. tba
Corpus Christi, Nov.tba
Washington DC, Oct
Ft. Lauderdale, Sept tba
Detroit,. Sept tba
Minneapolis, Sept tba
St. Louis, Sept tba
Las Vegas, Sept tba

COMMUNITY ORGANIZATIONS CONFERENCES AND OTHER EVENTS

ACT NOW , Chicago, Apr 22
AIDS, Sixth Intrnl Conf. on, San Francisco, Jun 20,
AIDS Candlelight Vigil, May 20,
AIDS Center of Queens Co., Jun 1,
American Gay Atheists, Apr 13, June tba
Arkansas Gay & Lesbian Task Force Aug tba
Bar Assn. Awards Dinner in New York, Mar. tba
Big Men's Convetion, Sep 1
BiPOL Jun 21
Black & White Men Together
Baltimore, May 4
Cleveland, Nov tba
Detroit, Jan 26
Indianapolis, Sep 1
Memphis, Jan 26
Philadelphia, Mar 2
San Francisco, Jun 24
TBA May 25
Washington,DC, Oct 5
Black Gay & Lesbian Leadership Forum, Feb 14
Colorado Gay & Lesbian Task Force Oct.tba
Committee of Black Gay Men,Oct 26
Federation of Parents & Friends of Lesbians & Gays, TBA
Four States Community AIDS Project, April tba
Gay Activist Alliance in Morris Co., N.J., Apr 28
Gay Asian Conference, Bangkok, Aug 24
Gay Youth Community Coalition, Jun 15
Gay/Lesbian Parents Coalitian Internat'l, Jan tba, March tba, Jun 1, Jun 2
Girth & Mirth of Greater S.F., Jun 2
Health Conferences
Washington DC, Jul 18
Missourl, Jun tba, Aug tba
Homosexual Information Center, july tba
Horizon's Gay/Lesbian Identity Conference in Chicago, Oct. tba
Leadership Conf. Black Lesb/Gays, Feb 15
Louisiana Gay & Lesbian Conf., Jun 15,
National Assn. of Black & White Men Together Jun 24,
National Coming Out Day Oct. 11
Natl Gay & Lesbian Task Force, Leadership Conf. erence, Nov 9
North American Man/Boy love Assn, Oct. tba

P.F.L.A.G. Oct 12
Political fundraisers:
Chicago, Feb 18
San Jose, Apr 7
Southeast Conf. for Lesbians/Gays, Mar 22
Stonewall Union, Columbus, Aug 2, TBA
Words Project for AIDS, TBA

CONCERTS

Boston , Mar. 11, Mar 17, June 10, Jun 15
Chicago, Mar 24 Jun 16, Dec. tba
Denver, Apr 7, Apr 28,Jun 23,Dec 9,
Des Moines, Apr 1, Jun 23
Ft. Lauderdale, June tba
Honolulu, June, Dec tba
Long Beach, June 9
Minneapolis Apr 7, Jul 21
Philadelphia, April, Dec tba
Portland, Apr 14, June 23, Dec 2
Santa Cruz, Feb tba
Washington, DC
Mar, 30, Dec. tba, June 16

CONTESTS

California State Prelims:
Ms. California Lady-of-the Year (Lesbian)
Mr. Gay California
Ms Gay California/America (Female impersonator) TBA
International Mr. Leather, May 25
Mr. Gay Columbus, Mar. 26
Nationals TBA:
Ms Lady-of-the -Year
Mr. Gay All-American
Miss Gay America

CRUISES

(Day) Philadelphia, Aug tba
(Day) Philadelphia, July tba
Caribbean, Feb.18, Mar 4, May 27, Jul 1, Oct 28, Oct. tba,
Caribbean (Women) Feb., Oct 28
French Canada, Jun 30
Greece, Aug 26
Greece, Sept. 2
Key West Party Cruise, Oct.26, Oct 27
Mexican Riviera, Mar 24
Mexican Riviera (Women), Nov 17
Yucatan, Mar 10

FAIRS & FESTIVALS

Film festivals:
Key West, Fla., June tba
Minneapolis, Mar 29
San Francisco, Jun 15
Folsom St. Fair, San Francisco, Sept. tba
Pioneer Days, So. Calif., Oct. tba
Street fair, W.Hollywood, Oct, tba
Street fair, Denver, Jun, 2

HOBBY GROUPS

Science fiction, Tewksbury MA, Jul 20
Dark Shadows Fan Club, Los Angeles, Oct 31
Stamp collectors, New York City, TBA

PRIDE CELEBRATIONS

Chicago, June 24,
Columbia, S.C., June 23
Columbus OH, June 16
Denver, June 23
Long Beach, May 19
Milwaukee, June 16
Minneapolis, June tba
New Orleans, June 23
New York City, June 24
Philadelphia, June 3
San Francisco, June 24
St. Louis, June 24
W.Hollywood, June tba

PROFESSIONAL MEETINGS

AIDS Health Project, Jan 17, Feb 1
AIDS Intern'l Conf. in S.F., June 24
American Library Assn., Gay/LesbianTask Force, Jun 23
Assn of Gay/Lesbian Psychologists, TBA
Assn. for Gay, Lesbian, & Bisexual, Issues in Couseling, Mar 16
Assn. of Gay & Lesbian Psychiatrists, May tba
Colorado AIDS Project, Feb 1
Gay & Lesbian Press Assn., May 4
Gay Public Health Workers Caucus TBA
Intern'l Gay Travel Assn., May 16
Lesbian, Gay, Bisexual People in Medicine, Mar. tba
Natl Lesbian & Gay Law Conference, June 6
Women and the Law Conference, Mar. tba

RELIGIOUS GATHERINGS

Affirmation/Methodists, Apr 12, Sep 15
CHUTZPAH Toronto, June 29
Congregation Etz Chaim N. Miami, Apr 10, Sept. 2, Sept. 29, Sep 30
UFMCC Clergy Conference & Great Lakes Dist, Oct 17
Spirituality/Theology Consortium, L.A., Oct. 26
Jewish Lesbian Daughters of Holocaust Survivors, TBA
MCC Eugene, Oct tba Dec 1
MCC Huntsville, Apr 15,
MCC Key West. Nov 22, Dec 24
Presbyterians for Lesbian & Gay Concerns, TBA, Mar 2, May 27, May 29

Reconciliation MCC
Grand Rapids, Mich., Oct. tba, Sept. tba, Feb 28, Apr 12, Apr 13
Apr 15, May 25, June 17, Dec 5, Dec 24
Unitarian-Universalists for Gay/Lesbian Concerns, Feb 16, June 16
World Congress of Gay & Lesbian Jewish Orgs.,TBA, Apr 28, June 29

RODEOS

Phoenix, Jan 12
Seattle, Feb 18
Denver, June 29
Wichita, Jul 20
Finals TBA, Oct. tba
Los Angeles, Mar 30
Oklahoma, May 25
Texas, Nov 16

SOCIAL EVENTS (DINNERS, DANCES, PARTIES)

Atlanta, Aug 4
Bethany Beach DE, May 26, Jul 4, Sep 1
California, Sept.tba
Chicago, Mar 31
Columbus OH, Sept. tba
Hunstville Ala, Aug. tba, Sept. tba, Dec 23
Kalamazoo, Mich., Feb. tba, July tba
Long Beach, Mar 4
Maplewood NJ, Mar 17
N. Miami, Mar 10, May 12
Newark, NJ, June tba
New York City (Seniors), Jan tba, June tba
Oakland CA, May 26
Oregon, Oct 27, Dec 22
Philadelphia, April tba, March tba, Sept. tba
San Francisco Girth & Mirth, Feb 10, Mar 24, Apr 28, Jul 28, Sep 22, Sep, Oct 27, Nov 24, Dec 22, Dec 31, Dec. tba

SPORTS

Body building, San Francisco, June 23
Cycling
San Francisco, May 12
Denver, June 30
W.Hollywood, April tba
Gay Games III, Vancouver, Aug. 4
Motorcycle, No. Calif., Jul 28
Softball
Pittsburgh, Aug 19
Milwaukee, May 25
Skiing
Aspen, Colo. Gay Week, Jan 20
California, Jan 19, Feb 16, Mar 23
Colorado, Jan tba, Feb tba, March tba, April tba, May tba, June tba, Nov tba
Lake Tahoe. Feb. tba
Tennis
Seattle, Apr 25
San Francisco, May 26
San Diego, Jun 30
Walking
Denver, Sep 23
Long Beach, Mar 12

SQUARE DANCES

Albuquerque, Oct 13
Atlanta, Oct tba, Dec. tba,TBA
Calif, Sept. tba
Chicago, Sept. tba
Cleveland, July, Oct. tba, Dec. tba
Denver, TBA
Florida, March tba
Los Angeles, Feb 16
New York City, Feb tba, Jun 25, Jul 4, Oct 26, Dec tba, TBA
Philadelphia, June tba
Phoenix, Jan 12, Feb tba
Portland OR, Apr 7
Rehoboth Beach DE, May 18
Russian River, Feb 9, April tba
Sacramento, TBA
San Francisco, Mar 17, June 23, TBA
Seattle, Jan 1, Feb 16, Apr. 10, Jul 28, Sep 1, Oct 5
Toronto, TBA
Vancouver, Apr 12, Aug 25, Nov 23
Washington, DC, Nov tba

TOURS & TRIPS

Calfifornia Apr tba, Aug tba July tba, June tba
Ontario Canada, June tba
Everglades, Fla, March tba
Grand Canyon, May tba
Reno NV, Jan 27
Yosemite, Jun 8, Jul 6,
Russian River, Aug 25
Hawaii, Mar 13, Apr 18, Apr 21, Aug 13
Oregon, Jun 2, Aug 10

ADVENTURE TRAVEL

BikeTrips:
Africa, Nov 30
France, Jul 15
Nova Scotia, Jul 19

Canoe Trips for Women:
California, Apr 1
Minnesota, Jun 29, Jul 14, Jul 15, Jul 28, Aug 12, Sep 9
Quetico Country,Aug 6

Climbing for Women
Alaska, June tba
Washington State, Apr 22, Apr 28, May 5, Jun 9, Jun 16, Jul 8, Jul 11, Aug 11, Aug 18, Sep 8, Sep 22,
Minnesota, Jan 31

Dogsledding for women
Minnesota, Jan. 31

Hiking Trips:
Washington State, Mar 3, Jul 29
Swiss Alps, Aug 6
Nepal, Apr 20

Scotland, TBA
Utah, Apr 30

Kayak Trips for Women
Baja, Feb 10, Feb 17, Apr 21

Llama pack trips for women, in Oregon, Jul 21, Sept. 3,

Men's Tours
New Zealand, Jan 26
Costa Rica, TBA
Macchu Piccu, TBA
Nepal, TBA

Rafting:
Oregon, Jun 17
Washington, Jan 20, Feb 19, Idaho Aug 7

Ski Trips:
Aspen, Jan 20
Idaho, Mar 10
Washington State, Jan 13, Feb 2, Feb 9, Feb. 10, Mar 2

Women's Tours:
Africa, Jan 21, Jul 22
Alaska, May 20
China, Apr 30, Jul 28
Costa Rica, Feb 26, Mar 12
Cozumel, Mar 13, Mar 20
Crete, Sep 7
Mexico, Feb 25, Nov 21
Minnesota, Feb 16, Mar 1
Nepal, Mar 31, Nov 10
New Zealand, Feb 12
Northwest, Aug 12
Peru, June 20
Puerto Rico, Apr 28
Ptarmigan Transverse, Jul 22
Puerto Rico, Apr 21
Russia, Oct tba
Sikkim, Mar 12
Thailand, Feb 3
Tibet, Oct tba
Washington State, May 12, Jun 2, Jul 8, Jul 15, Jun 23, Aug 5

WOMEN'S GATHERINGS
(Also see Cruises, Tours & Trips)

Dinah Shore Golf Tournament in Palm Springs, Mar 28
Old Lesbians Planning Meeting, TBA
Radical Women's Conference in Los Angeles, Feb 17
Wimmin's Spirituality Festival , Oxford Pa, May 18
Music Festival, Oxford Pa, May 24
Michigan Women's Music Festival, Aug 8
East Coast Lesbian Festival, Sept. tba
Women Artists Exhibit in W.Hollywood at City Hall, Jan 1
Women's History Month Events in West Hollywood, Mar 1
Women's Leadership Seminars:
Minnesota, Jun 8
Washington State, May 12, Jul 8, Aug 8, Sept.16, Oct 6
Southern Women's Music & Comedy Festival in Georgia, May 24
Golden Threads celebration of older lesbians in Provincetown, June 22
West Coast Women's Music & Comedy Festival in California, Aug 30
Women's Dance in San Francisco, Dec. 31
Nat'l Women's Music Festival in Blooming ton, Ind., June tba
Lesbian Dance in Chicago, TBA